Praise for *Embracing Uncomfortable*

When someone is able to make complicated topics simple, I always listen! And that's exactly what Dr. Deb does. Not only does she walk us through what she knows, she lives out her words and that's more important to me than any knowledge she possesses. I'm so excited for this book to get into the world!

BIANCA JUAREZ OLTHOFF
Teacher, preacher, and bestselling author of *How to Have Your Life Not Suck*

Why is it so easy to get knocked off course and so hard to say "no" to the things that keep us there? Enter this incredible book. Perhaps the best book I've read, period, to powerfully guide someone out of the easy places and choices that get us nowhere. And to guide us instead through the "uncomfortable" places. The ones that really can bring genuine change toward what we really want and need most in life. Life is hard. This book can show you how to quit making it harder and actually reach those places of purpose, happiness, and rest you thought were out of reach.

JOHN TRENT
President, StrongFamilies.com; author of *LifeMapping* and coauthor of *The Blessing*

Some messages come to us too late, others may come too early. In these pages is a message right on time. You cannot overcome what you are unwilling to encounter. Just how to do that is the gift Dr. Gorton bequests to us in this expertly written narrative *Embracing Uncomfortable*. Read it and rejoice.

CHARLIE DATES
Senior Pastor, Progressive Baptist (
affiliate professor, Trinity Evangelic

D1490553

If you want to wake up every morning with a sense of purpose, you have to live ON purpose. Being intentional in that way means truly knowing what your purpose is. Deb Gorton is here to help with that!

ANITA PHILLIPS, LCSW-C
Founder, Turn the Light On Movement

Even though we may know God has a plan and purpose for our lives, many of us will forgo our purpose in order to remain in our comfort zone. In *Embracing Uncomfortable*, Deb Gorton invites us to push beyond our fears. She helps us to discover what is keeping us from our purpose and provides us with realistic solutions that will move us into our purpose zones. This book equips us with the tools we need to make our daily pursuit of purpose our lifestyle.

KIM ANTHONY
Author, speaker, host of the *Unfavorable Odds* podcast

EMBRACING UNCOMFORTABLE

Facing Our Fears While Pursuing Our Purpose

DEBORAH E. GORTON

NORTHFIELD PUBLISHING

CHICAGO

Some content in chapters 5, 7, 8, and 9 was adapted from the author's blog posts.

All stories involving clients have been altered and references are a combination of
various stories to protect confidentiality.

All Scripture quotations, unless otherwise indicated, are taken from the New American
Standard Bible®, Copyright © 1960, 1962, 1963, 1968, 1971, 1972, 1973, 1975, 1977,
1995 by The Lockman Foundation. Used by permission. (www.Lockman.org)

Edited by Elizabeth Cody Newenhuyse
Interior and cover design: Erik M. Peterson
Cover illustration of pencil pattern copyright © 2015 by CSA-Printstock / istock
(465531316). All rights reserved.
Author photo: Patricia Martinez

Library of Congress Cataloging-in-Publication Data

Names: Gorton, Deborah E., author.
Title: Embracing uncomfortable : facing our fears while pursuing our
    purpose / Deborah E. Gorton.
Description: Chicago : Northfield Publishing, 2020. | Includes
    bibliographical references. | Summary: "We face thousands of choices
    between what is best and what is easier. When you learn to embrace the
    uncomfortable as a gateway to better things, everything changes.
    Discover the freedom that will fill your life when you begin to see
    discomfort as an important step toward reaching your goals"-- Provided
    by publisher.
Identifiers: LCCN 2019059133 (print) | LCCN 2019059134 (ebook) | ISBN
    9780802419569 (paperback) | ISBN 9780802498458 (ebook)
Subjects: LCSH: Goal (Psychology) | Self-actualization (Psychology)
Classification: LCC BF505.G6 .G67 2020 (print) | LCC BF505.G6 (ebook) |
    DDC 158.1--dc23
LC record available at https://lccn.loc.gov/2019059133
LC ebook record available at https://lccn.loc.gov/2019059134

We hope you enjoy this book from Northfield Publishing. Our goal is to provide
high-quality, thought-provoking books and products that connect truth to your real
needs and challenges. For more information on other books and products that will help
you with all your important relationships, go to northfieldpublishing.com or write to:

Northfield Publishing
820 N. LaSalle Boulevard
Chicago, IL 60610

1 3 5 7 9 10 8 6 4 2

Printed in the United States of America

To my mom.
You knew I had this in me long before I ever did.
I miss you every day.

CONTENTS

FOREWORD

By nature, most of us relish the "comfortable"—until we realize that being comfortable does not always move us to our desired goals. I remember a young man who aspired to be a pilot, but he could not bring himself to leave his comfortable job and obtain the necessary training. Thus, he never became a pilot. Most physicians will acknowledge that medical school is not comfortable, but it is necessary if one is going to become a medical doctor.

To walk the "easy" road is ultimately impossible. Whether we have clear purpose and values, or simply are wandering without direction, difficult times will find us. How we respond to the uncomfortable times will greatly impact whether or not we will reach our potential in life.

Those who choose to run from the uncomfortable will likely wake up in an even more desperate situation. On the other hand, those who choose to embrace the uncomfortable, seek wisdom, and courageously walk through the pain will likely see the sun shine just beyond the present darkness.

When we face uncomfortable circumstances, discovering our

purpose and values will greatly enhance our ability to make wise decisions. Without this clarity, we are left to our emotions of the moment, or to the advice of our peers who are also living without purpose and values. In this book, Dr. Deborah Gorton offers practical guidance for clarifying your purpose and values.

With these clearly in mind, you will be equipped to make wise decisions when faced with uncomfortable challenges. You will learn how to filter your emotions through the sieve of reason. Identifying your emotions is important, but more important is discovering the source of those emotions. Identifying the root from which our emotions emerge helps us evaluate their importance. We are all influenced by our emotions, but we need not be controlled by them.

Reading this book is like sitting with a seasoned counselor who wants to help you make the most of your life. You can embrace the "uncomfortable" seasons in your life.

GARY D. CHAPMAN, PhD
Author of *The 5 Love Languages*®

INTRODUCTION

The hardest season of my life started when I was twenty-nine years old. My mother passed away unexpectedly, and the things that happened in my family—and in my own life—afterward challenged the expectations I had held for the way relationships, decisions, and our pursuit of purpose should be approached. Growing up much older than my sister and brother, I looked forward to the time when my siblings caught up to me in the adult department, and our collective family relationships shifted closer toward the context of friendship and away from the framework of caretaking. I dreamt of the day when my parents no longer labored under the daily practical responsibilities of raising kids, and we could enjoy the experiences of celebrating one another's milestone life achievements—getting married, having kids, buying the first house. Being adults together.

But when my mom died, that dream shattered. What I didn't recognize at the time, and it took nearly a decade to fully unpack, was that my entire concept of how to navigate life shattered too. The pursuit of an idealized family represented a deeper perspective: that my ultimate goals were wrapped up in the context of comfort. The relationships, decisions, and purposes I was chasing after signaled an ultimate desire for safety and a greater ease in life. Family, the way mine lived it out, was **hard** (I'm sure no one can relate to that). The family I dreamt of would be *easier*, more *comfortable*.

Of course, I could easily argue that this dream was and is a wholesome, healthy one and is commonly shared by most people at some point in their lives. This is true! In fact, in the years that followed my mom's passing, as I came to learn more about my motivations and perspectives, I could say that this longing is still very real and present for me. It's what that picture looks like and my role within it that's changed drastically. What I've come to understand is that without careful consideration of the *why* behind the dream, the impact of living without the *why* is a daily pursuit of comfort that is incongruent with our core values and overarching purpose.

Life is never consistently easy. Family is never consistently easy. I'm not a consistently easy person to be around. But deep down I didn't want to live the *easy* life; I wanted to live the *me* life, the one that authentically aligned with my values and purpose. And that was always going to require a willingness to step into uncomfortable spaces. If I valued relationship, a #2 core value (we'll get to those later), a close-knit, healthy family dynamic made sense, but what did that look like in my everyday decision-making? Some days it meant sacrificing comfort, the things *I* wanted to do, for the uncomfortable—the well-being of others. Some days it looked like the uncomfortable task of confronting my attitude or choices in recognition of the hurt they caused others, instead of the comfortable choice to justify my attitude.

Here's the thing: while in the moment these were never easy

actions to take, the resulting *outcomes* always left me feeling a greater sense of long-term peace.

Enter epiphany number two. While I had always seen the specific details of my future goals as helpful to their accomplishment, those details actually derailed my decision-making more frequently than I realized because I was locked in to a specific outcome and didn't know how to navigate life when it changed (especially when I had no input into the change). When my mom died, and the destination I was charting changed drastically, I had no idea what to do. Instead of being purposeful, my decisions became reactive. And while crisis will always shift us off course in some way, I don't believe that shift had to be as dramatic as it was had I been fully in tune with what were the more critical keepsakes in my personal ecosystem. Starting each day with an intentional consideration of my values helped me to see where I was defaulting to comfort instead of persisting through the uncomfortable to gain what was in line with who I was created to be and what I desired most. In fact, going further and surrendering my focus on the bigger picture to the attention of everyday decisions actually served to draw me *closer* to what was most important to me.

Writing this book has reminded me of the transformational impact of knowing our values and consistently choosing to push through the barriers that prevent us from choosing, living, and thriving out of them. My hope is this book will do the same for you. I'm cracking open some vulnerable places along my journey to invite you into a conversation that shares a common thread in all of us, the desire to pursue and live according to our deepest values and true purpose. From my experience and the invitations I've received to step into the experiences of others, this necessitates a willingness to embrace uncomfortable. So, to help you along the way I've started each chapter with a definition that captures the essence of the content discussed in that section and a question with the goal to inspire your active participation in the process. Embracing uncomfortable is a journey we can't and weren't designed to do alone. I'm humbled and honored that you've let me join you.

1

THE COMFORT MYTH

com·fort myth | \ ˈkəm(p)-fərt ˈmith:
failing to live according to our core values and
true purpose by defaulting to the familiar, aka comfortable.

*What have you sacrificed in your life, whether intentionally or
unintentionally, that has prevented you from fully living a life
that represents your purpose and your identity?*

When I was in graduate school the pinnacle of our learning experience was assessed by a test called the "comprehensive exam." Exactly as the name implies, this all-day experience was like the Ninja Warrior of psychological knowledge appraisal. You could take the exam at any point in the first four years of your studies, but it had to be passed by the time you started the internship application process at the beginning of year five. Ever the achiever, I started early . . . like *really* early. We're talking first year, first semester.

I should mention that my psychological knowledge at this point was comprehensively limited to my run-ins with celebrity types during my brief employment at NBC Studios in the non-prime-time publicity department (another story for another chapter). Did I have experience? Yes. I was working with celebrities! Did I have knowledge? Well, I could tell you that Freud had an ego. And everyone blames their mother.

Needless to say, I failed. Yet, ever determined to succeed and succeed early and often, I persisted and took the test again six months later.

Fail.

Another six months later.

Fail.

Maybe a year will help.

Fail.

To date, I'm confident I've set some unattainable record with my graduate school for "most likely to stubbornly insist on passing this devil-of-a-test."

Seven times. That's how many tries I had before I finally passed that miserable exam. Over five years of failures, during which professors suggested I reevaluate my goals (believe me, as a professor now I would be telling my students to do the same thing!), I went to the one therapy session I could afford at the time in hopes that there would be some magic cure for the growing anxiety I was now experiencing on a regular basis.

I can confidently say that for most of the six years I studied for my PhD, nothing ever felt "right."

Fast forward to three months later, I missed passing by a handful of points. After one failed attempt, my blessed tribe of graduate school friends found me wandering the streets of Pasadena, milkshake in hand, tears and snot running down my face. They embraced me as I hiccupped my way through a sobbed recitation of professed inadequacies. With their ever-persistent encouragement and support, I gave it another go. Result: failed by a single question.

DO YOU REALLY BELONG HERE?

I'd never been confident of my choice to pursue a graduate degree in clinical psychology (likely a big factor in my repeated failure of that nightmare test). I think we all have that single question that tries to keep us from achieving what we have set out to accomplish, and this was mine: *"Do you really belong here?"* I didn't see myself as an academic thinker (and often still struggle with that one—doesn't God have a sense of humor). I was more inexperienced than all my peers, coming from a creative writing background and practical expertise in the wrangling of famous people. An art form, sure, but it was definitely a stretch to find a crossover in skills application.

I was certainly unclear about the direction I hoped to pursue with my degree and only seemed to gain less clarity as time went on. Every step in the direction of my degree felt more like an obstacle than an open door. I had to take additional classes to meet the program's application requirements. Finally, when I did apply, I was waitlisted* with discouraging feedback that I wouldn't likely receive acceptance. Then, when I finally did get in, there she was, four-hundred-and-something empty bubbles waiting for me, the dreaded comprehensive exam. I can confidently say that for most of the six years I studied for my PhD, nothing ever felt "right."

During those six years, I would have quickly admitted that school was challenging because I didn't believe I fit in. Yes, the DEFINITELY did not help with that; however, in retrospect the

---

* Waitlisted: One of the most uncomfortable realms to be in. Basically, where many of our hopes enter hospice care to transition slowly to death.

greater issue was so much deeper. If I were to place myself in my shoes back then I would easily say my expectation was to fall into the ideal identity of a standard graduate student; to achieve high marks on my exams and papers, be seen as a deep, intellectual thinker, to have professors expect and anticipate serious achievement levels from me, and to be comparable, better yet *compatible*, with the aspiring abilities of my fellow classmates. If I could be all those things, I would feel *comfortable*—that I fit, because I had unconsciously determined that this fit provided me the assurance that I was worthy of being there. That I *belonged*. Yet in all honesty, the deeper truth was that I felt like a fraud in most of those areas. I felt like a fraud in a room full of Freuds, and that stupid standardized exam wasn't helping.

So why did I keep taking the awful thing? People often ask me why I didn't give up on that test after failures number 2–6. Here's the ultimate irony: the answer is, because of my *fear of failure*.

(Come again??) I'd committed to doing a PhD, told everyone I knew I was doing a PhD, and was now filtering all my major life decisions through the lens of "once I finish my PhD." I'm the first official case study for embracing uncomfortable. While failing that test over and over was one of the most miserable experiences of my life, the thought of *not* passing it was not a reality I was willing to readily accept, because I had unconsciously placed my identity in overcoming it. Other options were simply . . . not an option.

> Every endeavor I pursued was designed to move me in the direction of what I *thought* I wanted to be, or more accurately, how I wanted to be seen.

Again, that word *fraud* was the key. To see oneself as a fraud suggests that your core identity is one of an impostor, a fake. That could not have been truer of the better part of my graduate school career. Every endeavor I pursued was designed to move me in the direction of what I *thought* I wanted to be, or more accurately, how I wanted to be seen. If I could achieve what I perceived my classmates as pursuing, accomplishing, and excelling in, I would fully embrace the role I had defined for myself and the expectations I believed should come with it. (Take note of that "should"—we'll come back to it later.) I would grant myself permission to *perceive* that I fit in. What that meant was that unconsciously I also believed something entirely untrue—that once I achieved that status, I would experience a great sense of belonging and, as a result, an overwhelming feeling of comfort. What a terrible myth. I was trying to mold my identity into this misconception that would cocoon me and ultimately give me the wings that were purposefully going to set me free. Unfortunately, what was supposed to set me free was keeping me in bondage. Or more accurately, here I was in this cocoon expecting to come out as a butterfly when I think I was really created to be more of a seagull.

TRYING TO MEET OTHERS' EXPECTATIONS

One might argue that the expectations I had of the typical graduate student weren't really that off, and that's probably true. The catch is, deep down those really weren't MY expectations. They were based on what I thought others expected of the role and of me in particular. I wasn't and never will be the academic who waxes philosophical in rhetoric as their main contribution to the development of their field of expertise. I'm a relator on every possible personality measure you can complete. I will nerdily admit

I love research, so I have that going for me. However, I always feel complimented when someone tells me I'm not the stereotypical image of what they expect a doctor/professor to be like. It validates who I truly am and who I am wholeheartedly not. Yet, for the better part of six years I was trying to be seen as that stereotypical misconception. If I were being brutally honest, I still am at times—more times than I'd like to admit. Because that's what we do. We live in a world of expectations that most of the time are based on what we think we *should* do, how we *should* behave, look, think, achieve.

BUT. These expectations are not consistent with what we really do value and desire to embrace—what could be argued as our purpose. We're so busy trying to live up to what we think the world expects, or to some image of ourselves, that we burn out. Then, we're too tired to actually live out what we want to live. Other people's expectations become

> Other people's expectations become our standard of living and one day we find ourselves disappointed and discontented.

our standard of living and one day we find ourselves disappointed, frustrated, stressed, discontented, exhausted (the list could go on) and wondering how the heck did that happen? Long story short, we're functioning in nothing close to comfort. How exhausting!

The kicker is, choosing to be that person we feel fully represents our purpose or identity often means going against the grain of what the greater culture defines as "right"—and that's also uncomfortable. Sometimes we become so weary of feeling like we're going against the grain that we just say, "What's the use?" When you're always playing defense, you're too worn out to play offense, and that's where the scoring actually happens! The choice of stepping into the discomfort of your authenticity despite the resistance you may encounter actually produces greater congruence and, ultimately, enduring comfort. It's the trade of short-term discomfort for long-term contentment instead of the other way around. It's challenging the myth of comfort in pursuit of daily living consistent with who you've been created to be.

THE WOMAN IN THE COFFEE LINE: A CAUTIONARY TALE

Well then, what prevents us from making this daily choice to embrace uncomfortable?

For one, our values are long-term, but our need to "feel good" is in the moment. We are prone to make an unconscious, reactive decision based more on a pattern of behavior instead of an intentional pursuit of the bigger picture of who we truly want to be.

I saw this in action not too long ago when I was waiting in line for coffee around the corner from my office. The customer in front of me was ordering the most preposterous cup of tea (picture Meg Ryan in *When Harry Met Sally*[1]—everything was customized and on the side. How one could do that with a cup of tea was nothing short of an art form). I was uncharacteristically not in a hurry that day and more fascinated by the cinematic tea production happening in front of me than any concern of where I needed to be next and when. I say that because how the woman behind me was responding could **easily** have been me on any given day, so I do not absolve myself of any responsibility here and I'm not judging her actions as beneath me. I'm just going to use them to illustrate a point because woman-behind-me was having a *moment*. You know those situations where someone makes a snide comment under their breath and then the emotion gets the better of them and their ability to modulate their tone of voice goes completely out the window? Woman-behind-me was in *that* place. She was huffing and puffing and grumbling so much she was basically live-commentating the tea-ordering fiasco of 2019 to the ENTIRE café. The thing is, if she'd stopped and thought about it, I don't think woman-behind-me would ever say she was trying to be the huffy, puffy, snuffy, grumbly individual she was presenting. I would buy stock in the fact that she wouldn't embrace those behaviors as part of her core identity or purpose; yet, here they were front and center. Her behavior was characteristically reactive. In the moment, she needed her experience of inconvenience to be validated more than her need to live congruent with her identity. Short-term comfort achieved at the expense of swallowing some pride, taking a deep breath, and considering what behaviors were more representative of her true character.

WHAT WE WANT, WHAT WE DEFAULT TO

This situation can apply to so many choices we make in life. It's the "what we want tos" verses the "what we default tos." Unfortunately, the defaults tos often fall in into the category of failure to act in accordance to our values. Try these on for fun-size.

- I want to spend more time with my family, but instead I maintain the same pattern of working overtime or over-committing to an abundance of activities.
- I want to be fully present in my marriage, but instead I give myself permission to get distracted by the less important stuff (this is a choose-your-own adventure-

style book, so you get to fill in the blank with what you define your own "less importants" to be).

- I want to eat healthier and be a better steward of my body, but instead I commit to busyness or anything that would help me avoid the requirement of getting up.
- I want to date someone who embodies the core values I desire in a mate, but instead I settle for whatever's front and center.
- I want to balance my finances according to my income, but instead I give in to my latest in a long string of impulse purchases.
- I want to live according to my values and purpose, but instead I default to the unintentional, reactive, habitual patterns that may feel comfortable in the moment but ultimately leave me feeling this sense of angst and lack of fulfillment because I never really arrive at where I want to be . . . or WHO I want to be.

We invite way too many "buts" to the decision roundtable. Here's where it's important to pause and clarify what the comfort myth actually is, because it's layered. The myth of comfort refers to:

1. The false identities, values, and purposes we're pursuing because we've convinced ourselves that's what we really want, without carefully considering the outcome's consistency with our core values.
2. The choices (which are genuinely yours) we make in the present that don't actually align with our authentic identities, values, and purposes because the experience isn't actually driven by a seeking of comfort but instead a default to familiarity.

Using my own story as a grad student, my comfort myth was that achieving the deeply philosophical and intellectual identity I believed a student *should* have would make me feel a great

> We invite way too many "buts" to the decision roundtable.

sense of comfort. Second, I was repeatedly choosing to take that exam over and over even though I clearly wasn't ready for it. Why? I thought passing that exam early on and with high marks would align me with Myth #1. So, Myth #2 was just perpetuating Myth #1!

I had two things going against me. I was pursuing a misaligned purpose AND failing anyway. My experiences were incongruent with my expectations (even if they were misaligned with what I really desired), and it left me feeling frequently and incredibly *uncomfortable.* I wish I knew then what I know now (no one's ever said that before), that the discomfort I was experiencing was not resulting from my failed attempts to live up to the image I'd constructed in my head, but actually a result of seeking false comfort* in choices that weren't congruent with my true values and purpose.

Social psychologists look at incongruence—when something isn't compatible with your expectations or feels out of place— as a byproduct of misaligned goals and unspoken motivations.[2] A broader use of the term, from a counseling perspective, is basically functioning in a state of experienced disagreement or inner conflict.[3] Navigating life circumstances, relationships, even basic daily choices, in a state of incongruence can lead to stress, anxiety, depression, diminished well-being, and poor mental health.

---

* Full disclosure: It's not in society's best interest to put "discomfort" on the labels of things. "Yes, your prom shoes are gorgeous, made out of Italian patent leather from only grass-fed alligators . . . and they'll also leave you pigeon-toed."

Yet often do we place ourselves, or find ourselves placed, in that category—not what I planned for, not my intention, not what I expected, nothing I can do about it?

For most of my graduate school career, I was smack-dab in the middle of a "not what I planned for" situation. I don't know that even now I could tell you what I *really* expected out of that time in my life, a time I'm **very** glad is now behind me. I can confidently tell you that even if I could articulate all this to you, it would be nothing close to what I actually experienced. And I think that's the problem. For five of the six years I was in grad school* I floundered around with a neglected focus on my purpose. Instead, I allowed my experiences to define me and my choices. These choices were habitual and automatic, not contemplated and intentional. So, when obstacles presented themselves like the Warped Wall on *American Ninja Warrior*, my responses were reactive and the perception I held of my identity shifted like a kite in the wind. I wasn't intentionally focused on my purpose. So, when something happened and I thought, responded, or behaved contrary to my core self, the outcome was often anxiety, frustration, disappointment, or despair. But I didn't know why.

Here's another example you might relate to. We live in a culture where the picture of a happily married lifestyle attained by a certain critical age is the Holy Grail of relational and life-status aspirations. For those of us who fall in the singles category, it's too easy to place the identity of "failure" in our bucket of labels. I've seen this comfort myth play on repeat in the lives of friends, clients, and family members. It goes like this: Myth #1: if I find the right person, aka my "soul mate," get married, and settle down

---

* Thank you for your purchase of *Embracing Uncomfortable*. 100% of the author proceeds of this book will go to the "Deb Gorton Student Loan Reduction Fund." Ha ha, just kidding. More like 5%. Your donations are greatly appreciated.

(what does that even mean!), I will feel fulfilled; I'll achieve a great feeling of comfort because I'll never feel lonely, inadequate, or unlovable ever again. Basically, these are the same qualities for a cozy throw or an R&B playlist. Or even if I do still feel those emotions, they won't be nearly as intense as they are now, *or* I'll have a permanent partner to soothe me out of any such feeling.

This myth also unconsciously suggests that I'm not adequate as a single and will never find true contentment and fulfillment in this stage of life, no matter what. This leads to Myth #2: DATE ANY BREATHING INDIVIDUAL THAT CROSSES MY PATH because being single is way worse than coupling off with some random dude or dudette. Who cares, as long as you're a couple!!

TRANSFORMATION IS POSSIBLE!

The consequence of living the comfort myth is an ongoing, restless desire for something else, because every time we achieve the false comfort we seek, it's never enough. Thankfully, transformation is possible! However, like I tell my clients (and inadvertently myself), saying it, recognizing it, that's the easy part. It's in the doing where things get difficult.

Notice, though, I said *difficult*, not impossible, and if we journey together our chances of success rise exponentially. So, to that end I'm going to be brutally honest about myself throughout this entire book, at the risk of exposing myself as the fraud that I fear I am. Why? Because it's critical we rise to this challenge together. Do you know that only eight percent of the general population actually takes the steps to meet the goals they set for themselves?[4] How do they succeed? They don't do it alone.

I get that! Over the last several years I've been blessed with an abundance of true, life-giving, intentional, honest, raw, vulnerable community. This is the type of community where I can be my gruesome, truthful, unfiltered selves (because I'm a "3" on the Enneagram I can default to many "selves" and still be fully loved and embraced). It's been in that intentionally created space where I've started to confront those destructive messages and move more into a fuller embrace of the momentary discomfort of choosing to be my authentic self—which leads to longer-term contentment and peace. It's in this space I've learned that everyone carries these messages, even those people with ten gazillion followers on social media who come across as having everything together. So, I want to do that for you. My prayer is that if I expose the truth instead of running and hiding from it, perhaps you'll feel the pull of bravery and gravitate toward doing the same and then turn and do so for others. So, the moral of the story is, find your people and commit to doing this work with them. It'll be your first practice in the art of stepping into the uncomfortable. (And yes, I'll be saying more about this "find your people" challenge.)

Once you've established the community that's going to journey with you in this process the next step is taking a long hard look in the mirror to determine where you're defaulting to the comfort myth at the expense of what you truly value. Recognition is always the first step toward transformation. We can't change what we don't know is there or we don't acknowledge as missing. So, pause with me for a second. Consider the hunches that are quietly nudging you toward an area of your life that represents a comfort myth (likely something habitual) versus a core value. It's okay if you're unsure

There's a reason the question "What's your gut telling you?" exists.

27

at the moment or if you haven't established what your core values are; we're going to address that process in another chapter. However, there's a reason the question "What's your gut telling you?" exists. The initial thoughts swirling in your brain as you've read the beginning pages of this book are the ones driven by unconscious emotion and are more likely to be consistent with what's authentically you. Sure, what you've jotted down may change considerably as you continue reading; however, it's also likely that you've established some key decisions here that won't change drastically but instead will go through the sieve of refinement as you navigate what follows.

Next, you need to carve out time, intentional time in your schedule to do this work. Block it off. Make it sacred to you and to others. I'll talk about the critical role of the discipline of pausing later on, but know you'll feel a greater sense of frustration in this process *without* a commitment to this time than the momentary discomfort of consistent, intentional pauses. These pauses serve to create the space necessary to evaluate progress (see how this cycle of discomfort to comfort is a part of nearly every decision we make!) and foundationally place us in a space of minimal noise and distraction.

Why do you think we so easily lose sight of our authentic purpose? Well, let me ask you this, when was the last time you actually thought about your purpose? Or, even better, have you ever sat down and thoughtfully, carefully, *intentionally* defined it? If you answered yes to either of those questions you've already graduated from *Embracing Uncomfortable* and should really be enrolled in *Embracing Uncomfortable 2.0*. Actually, why don't you just start writing it yourself (I'll take a 10 percent motivation and purpose fee from any and all future book sales). We lose sight of purpose because we never knew what it looked like in our own life to begin with, and we arrive there because we didn't take the TIME to honestly and investigate-ively (clearly, making up words is a pastime of mine) answer this question.

Most of us would probably say we're too busy. We offer the trite "there's not enough time in a day" answer, when ironically the discomfort of being too busy pales in comparison to the discomfort of functioning purposeless. To be clear, the choice to pursue purpose is one that will require frequent and costly sacrifices. However, the type of discomfort that comes from **those** losses, the ones that simply don't align with our fundamental values, is like the aching pain of a good workout—it yields a high return in the *long run*. Pun intended.

That's exactly what finally propelled me into a place of living more consistent with who I believed I was created to be rather than the created illusion of the self I was repeatedly failing to become.

I *DID* pass that exam and finally felt incredibly, overwhelmingly comfortable. FALSE! The day I finally passed was like the disappointing ending to an otherwise epic movie.* It felt kinda . . . blah. While I don't want to downplay the extremely hard work, persistence, and tenacity my graduate work required, I felt the same letdown when I walked across the stage to receive my diploma a year later. In fact, at that point I was finishing up a year of full-time internship where I was seeing about thirty clients a week and crying both to and from my daily commute to work, (yes, sometimes with a milkshake in hand). Things just didn't feel right. I had achieved what I set out to accomplish, but I continued to feel this nagging sense of discomfort in the outcome.

---

* Think *Titanic*—it was a grand and adventurous love story until that end scene with Jack slowly freezing to death in the water while we all knew there was PLENTY of room for him on that large floating door.

WHAT I LEARNED ON THE BEACH

A year later, I realized why during an unplanned forty days in the desert. Okay, my desert was a beach and forty days was more like ninety. Don't get any glamorous ideas, it was an East Coast beach in the dead of winter, so it was cold, and windy, and there was NO ONE around. However, thanks to my desolate surroundings my distractions were eliminated, and I was able to stop, look, and listen. I could actually engage in that critical practice of disciplined pausing. As I did so it allowed me to challenge the comfort myth by taking time to discern my false from true purpose.

Slowly, these false perceptions of who I wanted to be, how I wanted to behave, and where I wanted to go on my journey were gradually revealed. I began to see where my choices were causing me acute discomfort because they ultimately didn't align with most of who I really was. It wasn't just the false pursuit of an external mold that represented a professional, elbow-patched, tweed-wearing, philosophically thinking academician. There was more, a lot more.

I discovered I had to be the problem-solver in order to be seen as valuable. That I had to have the answers in order to be seen as competent. That I had to be in a relationship in order to be seen as worthy of something to offer based on the culture myth of my surrounding community. I could fill a chapter in this book with the insecurities I unearthed and the resulting behaviors I was engaging in that fought hard against the core of who I really was.

Here's the thing. After all this . . . I AM an academic. I'm currently running a master's in counseling program, serving as an associate faculty member, and was recently promoted to an endowed chair position. I don't say all this to toot my own horn but to toot that without any doubt, I KNOW I wouldn't be where I am today without a willingness to embrace uncomfortable things in order to fulfill the greater comfort of my calling.

Lest you think I have it all together, I've had to fend off the lure of myths since my days at the beach. They still catch me off guard, trap me in their sweet talk and conniving ways, and trip me up constantly. I'll even let you in on them if you continue reading.

The difference today is that I have a compass north. I know who I want to be, how I want to be, and where I want to be no matter my season or circumstance. This makes all the difference. I allowed myself to be stripped of the unnecessary to see that what I thought was beneath the surface was not really there at all. The shame, the discouragement, the uncertainty, the fear, the insecurity—those were feelings, but they were not and ARE not part of my identity. So, I stopped pursuing ways that suggested they were. Yes, that's uncomfortable, but the relief of being authentically me is so worth the momentary uneasiness of owning my insecurities and acting in opposition to them (more on this later one).

Now I want to help you do the same. The next chapters in this book are designed to steer you on a path (one we can journey together) of challenging the comfort myths in your own life. We'll explore the consequences of comfort and how embracing momentary discomfort can produce radical transformation in our lives. I'll walk you through some exercises that help to define our values and purpose in order to set ourselves back on course when we wander off track, and how to navigate the other bumps and detours we undoubtedly experience from time to time. If you're with me, all you have to do is turn the page.

Comfort.
Myth.
Challenge.
Accepted.

2

DRIVING AFTER WHAT'S IMPORTANT

in·con·gru·ence | \ in-kən-ˈgrü-ən(t)s:
the unpleasant feeling(s) we experience as a result
of the dissonance between the actual choices
we make in our daily lives and the ideal desire to
live consistent with our values and purpose.

*Purpose takes purpose. Where do you see your behavior
functioning contrary to where you want to be in life when it
comes to what is most important to you?*

Chicago. A city of nearly three million people. This is where I live. I didn't grow up in Chicago and I didn't move to this amazing city until well into my "adulthood" (placed in quotes because I rarely feel like an adult—plus I ate chocolate chip cookies for breakfast today so . . . you be the judge). That being said, I have fallen hopelessly and helplessly in love with Chicago. I love its architecture, its history, its people. It's a complicated love story with a complex and broken place that provides glimpses of redemption and restoration among decades in the cyclical process of wreckage and rebuilding. I have a long, long way to go before I truly earn the honor of calling Chicago home, but I work to make progress every day. One such way I purposefully invest in my city is walking as often as possible, even when Siri dutifully reminds me that the temperatures outside would suggest that I've transported myself to some arctic tundra. I walk to observe and reflect and know my surroundings. I walk so my neighborhood is familiar and my presence in it is focused on what is true, not what is ideal. I walk to work, to the store, to church, to the local coffee shop.

I'll be honest—walking here isn't always the most pleasant thing to do. Some days it's cold, some days it's hot. And humid— this Arizona girl did not know the meaning of humid until I started walking on a muggy summer day in the city. Some days it's dark, and some days, only some days, it's just right (it's like I'm Goldilocks and the Three Chicago Bears). In fact, I didn't start the practice of walking to work until recently, when my dad came for a visit and encouraged me to trek the two miles from home to my office as a way to get some exercise and give him the opportunity to explore the city while connecting with his daughter. The experience opened my eyes. As I took the same path week after week, long after Dad had returned home, I began to notice things I'd never seen before. It was like coming back to a favorite painting over and over again, only to notice new, undiscovered details as the larger, more visible elements slowly become familiar and fade into the background.

WALKING, VALUES, COMMUNITY

As I continued walking, I was struck with the realization that this new ritual was actually more consistent with my core values and defined purpose than my previous habits of bus riding, train taking, or more likely, rushing-out-the-door-Uber-requesting. Simply aligned, but aligned nonetheless.

Through a lot of contemplative practice, professional coaching, and disciplined reflection, I've come to a place of summarizing my purpose as "embracing uncomfortable in order to fulfill the calling of community." Along with that purpose are my five core values: Jesus, relationship, wisdom, authenticity, and purpose. Yes, a lot of my greater (think macro) decisions carry

> Walking daily in the city fell in line with pursuing community.

more significant weight on the application of my purpose and values, but I don't want to dismiss the smaller, micro decisions that provide the stepping-stones to the larger ones. Walking daily in my city fell in line with pursuing community (can you pursue community in a foreign space that you don't invest in knowing?) and is consistent with my values. It is a purposeful practice, enhances my knowledge of my surrounding community, and aligns with my commitment to steward my body well.

The choice to walk was and is a daily discipline. The warm covers of my bed, the promise of a slower start to my day, and the expediency of a faster commute via bus or train still calls to me most mornings. However, they are the comforts that yield a minimal return on investment. They're short-term comfort at the expense of long-term gain. How do I know this? Walking is consistent with my purpose; I fail to choose walking when I choose to walk away from that purpose and pursue habitual, reactive, or *easy* choices instead.

The choice to walk is also one I can afford to make and that is critical to recognize as well. Having a car is a convenience for me—not a necessity. It's a choice I can make that many others cannot. Pursuing our purpose means we have to be willing to sacrifice comfortable things. In my experience, most people don't define their purpose as "making everything in life about me and what makes me most comfortable." No, typically when we really consider our core purpose it has an outward, community focus that at least suggests a desire to contribute to the greater good. However, as we've already talked about, when it comes to aligning our *daily* choices with our core purpose, the opposite too often rings true, and our actions reflect a filter through the lens of "me" and rarely through the sieve of "others."

So my choice to walk is an intentional one. Other modes of transporting myself to work are honestly less conscious decisions and based more consistently on convenience. Yet, through the discipline of walking I've come to see that many of my daily choices stem from the later and not the former because walking also gave me the gift of reflection time. Without realizing it, I had carved out forty-five minutes of precious "solitude" in my day. I stumbled upon intentionality by making a choice that was more difficult but birthed a much greater outcome then I ever expected or intended.

Each of us has intentions—the way we desire to treat others, take care of ourselves, and navigate the world around us. Unfortunately, for many of us the outcome isn't consistent with the intention and we're left feeling the consequences of incongruence. Instead, we fall into the trap of engaging in common, unconscious behaviors, living the daily decisions of life without an intentional focus on choosing to consistently move toward our purpose. The list of reasons why can go on and on—once again that dreaded "lack of time," lack of energy, lack of motivation, too much anxiety. But the common theme among our excuses is almost certainly the fear of embracing uncomfortable. We're constantly defaulting to the myth of comfort.

Walk with me for a moment here. What is something you've wanted to accomplish but just haven't been able to? It might be treating your spouse with greater kindness and humility, stewarding the ways you take care of your body through a health and wellness lens, pursuing deeper, more meaningful conversations with your neighbors, or meeting your child where she or he is at versus where you want them to be. Now, consider the obstacles blocking your road to accomplishment, write them down in the margins. For most of us, every item on that list represents a discomfort, not an impossibility. (And if you think time is an insurmountable obstacle, keep reading. I have an answer to that I hope will shift your perspective.)

> What is something you've been wanting to accomplish but just haven't been able to?

Let me give you an example of someone who I believe was truly living out her purpose in life through the circumstances of what many of us might mistakenly characterize as meaningless or mundane. In those days of losing direction, feeling discouraged, insignificant, or lost—this is my story of hope.

"I'M JUST LIVING OUT MY PURPOSE"

Several years ago, before my discipline of walking, I hopped the bus on my way to work. On a typical day, one can expect a variety of interesting experiences on the CTA—Chicago's public transit system. I was once proposed to by a total stranger, and I've also learned the ins and outs of communicating a drug deal. Most of the time it's just a cramped journey with a fair amount of grumbling from tired, stressed out, or troubled passengers. However, this day was different from the moment I stepped aboard. Unlike the typical nod of a head I might get from a weary driver, I was greeted with an enthusiastic "welcome to my bus! I hope you have a blessed day and make sure to tell the person next to you it's going to be a beautiful day in Chicago today." I was pleasantly surprised, smiled at the friendly driver, and made my way to the back.

Her enthusiasm didn't stop there. Stop after stop she reminded each passenger of their worth and dignity by offering the same encouragement. Occasionally she got on the PA system and told us she was thankful we'd joined her on the journey today and to be grateful we're alive. After a few minutes of riding along, I had to make my way to the front and ask this woman what motivated her behavior. She didn't skip a beat in her response: "I'm just living out my purpose—making sure my passengers know they are seen and cared for on the short journey I get to share with them."

This driver wasn't curing cancer, or ending poverty, or (to my knowledge) amassing great amounts of wealth, things to which we typically (and I would argue *unfortunately*) ascribe greater dignity and purpose. According to the US Bureau of Labor Statistics (2017), bus drivers make just over minimum wage hourly and have higher rates of stress and on-the-job injuries than the national average. Yet, here was this woman, challenging what you might call the status quo of bus driver behavior by intentionally living authentic to her purpose no matter the circumstance. She wasn't bound by conditions or relationship status. From our brief conversation it was easy to envision her behaving in a consistent manner whether standing in the 10-items-or-less line at the grocery store behind an individual with an overflowing cart or discussing politics with a friend who holds starkly opposing views. Maybe she was wired with an extra dose of the friendly-in-all-circumstances gene; maybe I happened to catch her on the day she won MegaMillions before heading to work.

Maybe. But I happened upon that same driver a year later and I had the EXACT SAME EXPERIENCE. On an average weekday, 1.6 million people ride the CTA; she didn't remember me from Eve. Yet, her response was just as it was before: "Welcome aboard, you are special, thank you for being part of my journey today. You are blessed to be alive in this wonderful place."

I believe what set Bus Driver Betty (has a nice ring to it, doesn't it) apart from the people who drift through life in a chronic state of disappointment, discouragement, or discontent is a disciplined pursuit of purpose. She didn't lose sight of what was important to her—she drove after it, no matter the route and the conditions along the way.

GETTING OFF AUTOPILOT

Most of us function on autopilot. We might have some rudimentary understanding of who we want to be, what we want to accomplish, the legacy we strive to leave behind. However, our daily decisions often default to reaction not intention, and this ultimately leads to a lack of fulfillment and a general sense of failure.

This was what I was experiencing when I continued to miss those crucial points on that graduate exam. I was allowing an *actual* failure to define my identity and overshadow my purpose. The outcome was a constant feeling of inadequacy, disappointment, and loss. If I had been able to recalibrate my focus toward a deeply defined purpose that stretched far beyond the boundaries of this nuisance of an exam, my attitude and my actions might not have shifted so off course.

Notice I'm *not* saying my emotions would have shifted. Sometimes we get stuck in the false belief that aligning ourselves accurately with our purpose will eliminate all experience of unpleasant feelings. We'll cover that more in chapter 3.

We also fail to see how *all* our actions, down to the smallest, minute decisions, ultimately reflect what is most important to us. If you see your purpose as reflecting kindness to others, that should ring true just as much when you're standing in line at the DMV (or watching some poor soul order the most complicated cup of tea) as when you're ordering lunch from a stressed-out waiter while catching up with a friend.

I see this every day in my role as a therapist. Typically, at some point in my work with clients I come to land on this question of purpose, and I get all manner of responses. Some people (too many people) equate purpose with profession, and when they don't achieve their desired job status, or their work relationships lack fulfillment, they question their calling or their current situation. Others make purpose too complex—the unattainable holy grail of accomplishments. Mostly, people just don't take the time to think about their purpose and, with the best of intentions, they're now navigating life in direct opposition to the way they hoped and planned to. And why do people come to therapy? Because they're feeling all those emotions I mentioned in chapter 1 that come with an ongoing experience of incongruence: *not what I expected, not what I planned for, not my intention, nothing I can do about it.*

It's hard to start thinking about our purpose. When we do, we become aware of all the ways *we've failed* to align with our values, which often serves to multiply our already unpleasant emotions (I like to think of emotions like gremlins[1]—you get them wet and they just keep reproducing).

The beautiful thing is that I've witnessed and experienced firsthand how a disciplined consideration of our thoughts and behavior, sifted through the lens of our defined purpose, while momentarily uncomfortable, can lead to a more congruent and thus fulfilling life. We just have to learn to use uncomfortable to our advantage.

Most of us will feel uncomfortable multiple times in a day. If you don't believe me, pull out your phone (seriously, right now) and set a timer to go off every few hours. Let's go a step further and even label that timer "uncomfortable." When it goes off, I want you to pause and reflect on what's occurred in your life in the last hour or so. Did you react to a situation differently than you'd hoped? Did you make a choice that you regret (even something small like leaving for work later than you would have liked to or honking angrily at a careless driver)? Did you communicate with someone well on the surface while grumbling about them in your head? At the end of the day, reflect on the notes you've jotted down and circle the ones that are incongruent with your core values, even if you're not entirely sure what those values are yet. The goal here is to make uncomfortable conscious, because discomfort can actually be a valuable tool if we don't write it off and pretend it's not there.

We're too quick to write off emotions that we don't like . . . the, ahem, *uncomfortable* ones. Let's use an easy example to illustrate this point (easy meaning simple to understand, not necessarily to execute). You've put yourself out there in the online app store of dating options and your fishing pole has snagged a bite. Some flirty texts and a few phone calls later, you're set up for date #1. Several dates later, you've noticed some red flags. He's asked to crash on your couch and spot him a twenty because he's "in between jobs." Date #2 was at some random friend's birthday party and he left you alone most of the night while he mingled with his "guys." He mentioned hoping to receive his ninety-day chip at his next AA meeting.* In response, you justify away your concerns because deep down he REALLY IS a nice guy and is working on achieving his best self.

A QUICK LOOK AT JUSTIFICATION

If you're wondering how to spot a discomfort that signals an action misaligned with your values, justification is a great place to start. I'll say more about this later but here's a quick look.

Justification means we're having to convince ourselves that our actions aren't that bad. It's the behavior I utilize when I eat an entire box of Girl Scout Thin Mints because "at least now the box is empty, and I won't be tempted to eat any more." Never mind the 1200 calories I just scarfed down in one sitting. We don't justify good behavior, the behaviors that align with our values and purpose and actually bring us healthy comfort. There's no need to.

There's actually a psychological experiment that proves this point entirely. It's called the Theory of Cognitive Dissonance, and it was studied by two social psychologists at Stanford in the 1950s. Basically, these two dudes recruited participants to sit in a room for a few hours doing a really boring task, putting pegs on a board and turning them clockwise. After their participation, as incentive for volunteering some individuals were paid $20 to rate how enjoyable this dull task was. Surprisingly,

---

* Please note that I don't think there is anything wrong with dating a sober alcoholic. I applaud the hard work and persistent surrender that addicts go through day in and day out to stay clean. However, the rules of AA specifically state that distractions such as dating are seriously frowned upon during those critical first ninety days.

those who were paid a measly dollar for their time actually rated the exercise more positively than those paid the $20. Why? Justification. If I was willing to do this boring, bum-numbing task for a stinkin' buck it MUST HAVE been worth it.

Cognitive dissonance might as well be a synonym for uncomfortable and the treasure map to guide us to the root behavior is justification. If your value is a meaningful relationship with someone who's values and behaviors align with yours, why are you justifying dating Mr. Wrong-but-right-now? Because you've convinced yourself that the momentary comfort of companionship is worth the cost of long-term contentment. Unfortunately, you're just back in the cycle: what you hoped would bring you comfort is really just deceiving. Trust me, it's these kinds of choices that keep me in business.

Okay, it's kind of obvious that working for a dollar is a bad choice. Dating the wrong guy is a bad choice. But we justify those decisions because at some unconscious level we know they don't align with our values (we just can't bring ourselves to admit it). However, we can also engage in behaviors we don't feel the need to immediately justify because on the surface they DO align with our purpose and values but deeper below the inherent *motivation* does not.

I'll give you a personal example here. As I mentioned above, relationship is one of my core values and relationships carry the responsibility of my purpose (embracing uncomfortable to fulfill community—you give me an example of a relationship that wasn't uncomfortable). I'm the eldest child in my family of three; eldest by a lot (like, a mother's age). My Freudian slip is often referring to my siblings as my kids. Our mom passed away a number of years ago, so this urge is now even stronger. For all you moms of teenagers/young adults, you'll understand. The reaction to rescue, solve, and/or protect your kids doesn't stop once they leave the nest. To this day, if I get a call from my family, particularly my sister or brother, I can experience a great sense of guilt and anxiety if I'm unable to answer the call right there in the moment or I can't call back within a few minutes' time. I can become distracted in a meeting with a nagging sense of not being able to check in and see if everything's okay.

It's easy for that sense of discomfort to deceive me into thinking my priorities are out of whack and I'm pursuing achievement (aka work) over relationship. However, I've come to recognize many of these moments as motivated by a savior complex and not indicative of choosing inconsistent with my values and purpose at all. The discomfort is misleading, and I wouldn't be aware of that without the discipline of pausing and reflecting (and even more so, embracing the uncomfortable of allowing my community to speak truth into this area of my life!).

ASK YOURSELF . . .

Now I'm going to challenge you to do the same. Where are you living the comfort myth, losing sight of purpose, and justifying your actions because you've convinced yourself it's the only alternative and the outcome MUST be getting you closer to where you want to be? To help, I've found in my work and in my personal practice of challenging the comfort myth and embracing uncomfortable, there are three ways to easily lose sight of purpose:

1. Your purpose isn't applicable to all situations; instead, it shifts like the wind.
2. Fear is driving your behavior.
3. You struggle with a perceived lack of time.

Let's break it down. When it comes to *purpose*, as I mentioned before, too often we identify or unconsciously embrace specific motivations, as opposed to taking the time to define something more universal. We narrow the idea of purpose to vocational aspirations (my purpose is to be an influential CEO), relationship status (my purpose is to get married and have four kids), or accomplishments (my purpose is to run a marathon in every state). Instead, a broader purpose that applies in the smallest to the most significant areas of your life gives you the clarity and direction to challenge the comfort myth in daily decision-making and live more congruent to your values, just like Bus Driver Betty. In this way, it can be helpful to think of your defined purpose more like a life mission statement than a check mark on your to-do list.

Now let's talk about *fear*. In my opinion, fear and the other unpleasant emotions we encounter get a bad rap. If I had a dollar for every client that came into my office with the unconscious expectation that I would be able to essentially eliminate every experience of negative emotion from their life permanently, well, I wouldn't need to write this book and those pesky student loans wouldn't haunt me on a daily basis.

> We FEEL first, then put words to our feelings.

Emotions are a beautiful thing (yes, even the tough ones). They're the foundation of our decision-making. What's interesting about emotions is that they actually happen *before* we know what we're feeling. Emotions are birthed in the limbic system—basically the center of our brain.[2] **Then** they're defined with words through our cerebral cortex (that front part behind your forehead). So we FEEL first, then put words to our feelings. In a reactive situation where emotions are likely to be more intense, taking the time to consider how we're interpreting our emotions and in turn the meaning we assign to that feeling is often an afterthought at best and completely disregarded at worst. The consequence can then become sifting our emotions through the lens of lies.

Let's say you have the opportunity to take some type of risk but you're feeling apprehensive because you can't guarantee the outcome (so, basically 99 percent of life's decisions). The narrative in your head is: "I'm afraid because if I try this I might fail." That is a valid emotional experience based on what could be a very real possibility (I am afraid of doing stand-up comedy because there is a very real possibility I might fail at making people laugh). Every emotion we experience is valid (if you think differently, try *willing* yourself to feel something different the next time you wish you weren't feeling a specific emotion). So, my fear is valid. The reality of failing to make people laugh is also realistic.

Here's where things go south. Without a conscious boundary placed around those feelings and the consequential meaning of them, fear of failing becomes fear of failure and more specifically, fear of BEING a failure—as I mentioned happened to me when I was pursuing that awful exam. Instead of a feeling attached to an experience, now we've allowed the feeling to influence our perceptions and the outcome is embracing a false identity, one of being a failure. When we don't practice the disciplined pause that allows us to filter our emotions through truth, our behavior functions contrary to our purpose.* If we filter our emotions through an unhealthy lens, we begin to question our decisions, our abilities, and even our identities.

When it comes to *time*, chances are you don't have much of it, but as I mentioned above, I'm going to challenge the "impossibility" we attach to choices that require our time. We're all guilty of

---

* With fear, we often behave in one of three ways—fight, flee, or freeze.

claiming, "There just aren't enough hours in the day!" Yet you *know* we'd all be saying the same thing if we had a thirty-four-hour day. To use time wisely requires that we embrace the loss of something important for the greater gain of pursuing purpose. And we need to get creative and think outside the box. Remember, I added forty minutes of reflection time to my day, simply by choosing to walk to work! I have to get myself to work either way and the choice to walk only adds about twenty minutes to my commute time. The loss is more sleep but it's a lesser loss than the gain of those twenty minutes, which are quieter and more peaceful and private than the bus or train.

Maybe walking isn't an option for you, but I know there are other ways to create space in your day if you're willing to get creative and sacrifice some. Getting up ten minutes earlier might be a drag initially, but the rewards reaped could far outweigh the discomfort of that annoying alarm at 5:20. Working through lunch at your desk might be tempting as your "to-do" list piles up, but choosing to embrace the uncomfortable of "I'll get back to you" might result in greater clarity and consequently productivity later on. Always consider the cost of your actions.

Did you ever see the movie *How to Lose a Guy in 10 Days*?[3] There's a line at the end of the movie where Kate Hudson and Matthew McConaughey's respective characters are having their epic fight-before-they-fall-happily-in-love-ever-after scene. Matt yells, "You wanted to lose a guy in ten days, congratulations, you did it. You just lost him." Then Kate yells back, "No I didn't, Ben, 'cause you can't lose something you never had!" It's hard to lose sight of purpose if you've never taken the time to define it in the first place.

That's where we're off to next. It's time to embrace the Bus Driver Betty in all of us.

3

THE POWER TO CHOOSE

in·ten·tion·al | \ in-ˈtench-nəl de·sign | \ di-ˈzīn:
the launching pad of well-established values and purpose
we need to take radical steps in embracing uncomfortable.

Where do you need to intentionally design space
in your life in order carve out a truth-based definition
of your values and purpose?

Hunter S. Thompson, an American journalist, once wrote
that the tragedy of life is that we seek to set up and understand goals instead of taking the time to understand ourselves.[1]
He goes on to describe how a young child with dreams of becoming a firefighter will likely change his goals as he gets older, not
because the role of being a firefighter has changed but because
the child's perspective has. In other words, first, you have to know
yourself and strive to be yourself.

To me, this principle can be wholeheartedly applied to the
practice of stepping into the uncomfortable to pursue a purpose
that reflects our core values. It's the very essence of why I argue

that purpose should transcend our season and circumstance—because who we are is not limited by the situational factors that we encounter in living life. It's nothing more and nothing less than a daily choice. You and I have the power to choose.

QUESTIONS TO ASK YOURSELF . . . AND NOT TO ASK YOURSELF

Before you read on, this is a great place to pause and reflect. Consider the following questions and what immediate responses come to mind (nothing is wrong here—it all moves you forward on the journey).

Who am I today?

Who am I right now?

Who was I today?

Who does God say I am?

Daily reflection will shed light on who you are practicing to be and who you are choosing to become. The above questions should be on regular rotation as you consider what drives and grounds you.

The questions to avoid include:

Who is the culture saying I am? (That is, what are popular stereotypes about your profession, gender, age, faith, race, background?)

Who are my relationships (or lack thereof) saying that I am?

Who is my annual review saying that I am?

Who is my current vocational status saying that I am?

The answers to these questions are fleeting because they are based on what you produce instead of who you are. Who you *are* breeds purpose; what you *produce* bears witness to your purpose.

For example, if a core value in my relationships is connection, I may need to sacrifice my agenda in favor of listening to understand another person's views about something. But the outcome of deeper intimacy outweighs whatever result I sought to achieve from convincing the other person of my perspective. Conversely, this can act as a truth test. If you're not willing to sacrifice, then maybe connection isn't a true core value. That isn't to say you don't value connection; it's just not at the core of who you are. And that's okay.

WHEN I TRIED TO BE THE PERFECT CHILD

Before I dive deeper into the application and outcome of choice, that is, things we choose to do (or not do) in the moment, let me draw you an illustration of what it's looked like in my life, a narrative that is drawn not from my strength but from my struggle.

One of my most defining experiences is that I come from a family of adoptees. I have a sister and a brother, and we all birth from different adoption

> I always wrestled with the polarity of being chosen and being let go.

stories. It's one of my greatest joys to share this part of my identity and something that has significant influence on the woven tapestry of my life. However, I don't know if those of you reading this have been touched in some way by adoption and can resonate with this—but adoption is a beautiful story that can also come with a lot of pain. For me, I always wrestled with the polarity of being chosen and being let go.

I would say for the greater part of my childhood and adolescence my artificial purpose was in being the perfect child so I wouldn't lose out on this new family. This was an evil lie of a root that wove itself around my heart and my identity, this idea that I was expendable. As I stepped into emerging young adulthood, I had thoroughly grounded myself in the belief that my ability to solve, to fix, to take responsibility for, was what made me significant and worthy, what kept my place* in this family I treasured. In effect, in my unconscious core this is what I believed my purpose to be and what I consistently defaulted to (like rebooting to the basic factory settings when you do a hard restart on your smartphone because it's not behaving properly). Anything else was too uncomfortable. And this is where we get into the familiar notion of self-fulfilling prophecy.

The term refers to a concept often used in my occupational circle to explain why people get stuck in obviously unhealthy patterns of behavior. It's the idea that once someone holds a belief, no matter how destructive, about who they are, what types of relationships they're destined to experience and/or engage in, what opportunities they can anticipate, they unconsciously *seek out* ways to make these things a reality in their life despite the often-negative consequences. It's a sly and covert way that ongoing lies become a part of our story.

Others promote these lies too. Parents, friends, community, church, books, popular culture . . . someone or something is telling us, "This is who you need to be or what you need to do in order to be *needed.*"

For me, it wasn't far into my twenties that this lie started to really do its damage. The family I worked so hard to please, to serve, to sacrifice for because I was afraid of being cast out— that family started to unravel. My mom started to battle pretty severe mental illness. I was living a state away, struggling through

---

* Practical application: What keeps your place at the table, in your mind? What if what is keeping you "in place" is also what is keeping you from being at the tables that matter?

that insurmountable exam and oh, learning to be the epitome of problem solvers, and was also fielding consistent calls from Mom, my sister, my Dad, all requesting my interventions* in fixing the crumbling façade of our family's seemingly idyllic life. I was beside myself trying to figure out how to solve this heart-wrenchingly painful situation. When you establish yourself as the fixer, everyone turns to you for fixing. *Why* my parents turned to me and allowed my attempts at problem solving is a complex story that can best be understood in the reality that all families are complicated and dysfunctional from time to time. Just as we've had seasons of brokenness, we've also enjoyed and enjoy today beautiful seasons of healing and joy.

But at this particular juncture in my life, I wasn't prepared to fix, just like I wasn't prepared to take that exam. I was setting foot into a place before it was my time.

As this "fixing" was the purpose I'd misguidedly placed upon myself, the comfort of stepping into this role almost always won out against the challenge of pausing to consider truth.

Here's how that situation worked out. Two weeks after I walked across a stage and received my diploma, my PhD in Clinical Psychology—I was now crowned the problem-solver of all problem-solvers—I failed. Two weeks after I had been freshly minted the doctor of fixing all things unfixable, my mom chose to take her life, and my world came crashing down.

REBUILDING THE BROKEN FOUNDATION

How do you stay grounded when the purpose you are pursuing—a purpose motivated by the hope of being "chosen" that

---

* Who is intervening for you as you serve others?

had covered, albeit feebly, the fear of being unwanted and not enough—was now shattered in this decision you had no control over?

Now, before I go on, let me say that I love my mom very much. I have come to a place of healing and forgiveness, and the anger I once held is now a dulled sadness over the dark place she must have gone in those last years of her life. I also can't wait to dance and laugh with her again in heaven where her pain and darkness have been banished for eternity.

Let's just say for this impatient girl, God has taken His sweet time rebuilding—no, restoring—the broken foundation of my falsely identified purpose. In the time that's elapsed since my mom's passing, I've dealt with additional family tragedies, financial droughts, lost jobs, family crises, more moves than I can count, broken relationships, but also ongoing, life-altering transformation that started with a little seedling of truth planted deep in my heart.

An important confession here: I have since come to realize my entire understanding of the role of a psychologist was also greatly misguided by my misunderstood purpose. I cannot and will not be able to solve the problems of others (let's be honest, THANK GOD). As my authentic purpose became clear, the application to my occupational identity also shifted my understanding of the daily responsibility I bore in relation to the people I work with. I now see myself as called to listen with the goal of understanding and being non-judgmentally present with each person who walks through the doors of my office. *Not* fixing them.

But let's face it: that "fixer" purpose was familiar. Easy. I feared the outcome of stepping into the uncomfortable but authentic space of who I was created to be. I was always reacting to situations, rather than choosing, because the phrase that played on repeat during that season of my life was, "You don't have a choice." If my purpose was problem solving, any issue that presented itself was by definition mine to deal with. Unlike Betty (my bus-driving friend), I was functioning like a little silver orb in the pinball machine of my life, oblivious to the reality that who I was at my core could be equally applied in every situation. I had the power to choose, to be intentional, to do the work to figure out my true design and my true purpose.

Let me pause here and clarify something important. Choosing to assert your purpose in any circumstance doesn't minimize or invalidate the emotions you might be feeling. I was devastated when my mom passed. Regardless of seeing myself as the failed fixer or choosing to step into the uncomfortable to build the bridges of my community in a tragic time, I was always going to feel the searing pain and desperate loneliness of her passing. At no point in time do I want you, dear readers, to hear or believe that pursuing your purpose is done at the expense of your emotions. It's not about a trade-off. Take those emotions with you and be willing to let them help fuel your purpose.

> I was always going to feel the searing pain and desperate loneliness of my mother's passing.

WHAT I LEARNED ON THE BEACH, PART 2

Okay, so *how* did things change? At what point did the shift begin to tilt toward a more accurate understanding of my core values and purpose and the outcome of living accordingly? Well, if you, like me, have ever felt like a pinball than you know you can only take so many hits before something has to give. Remember the ninety-day beach challenge vacation I mentioned in chapter 1? Yep, this is the part of my story where, through a miraculous chain of events, I ended up living in the downstairs quarters of an elderly woman's beach house.

The circumstances in my life had left me feeling confused, uprooted, and stressed. My suffering was real and deep. And yet . . . my experiences had not destroyed me. I may have faced what I deemed to be my biggest fears—rejection and dejection—but I wasn't defeated. Yes, I learned in a very real way how what I had could be taken away in one day; how my circumstances could change in a second. Yes, I experienced the reality of my life like a fragile vessel. I was struck down at times, but the core of who I was had never been destroyed. The vessel I was using to fill and be filled? It just needed some serious remolding.

As I walked the snow-covered sand of the beach each morning, I began allowing myself to be stripped of the unnecessary to see that what I *thought* was beneath the surface, what I *thought* was my purpose, was actually never there to begin with. The shame, the discouragement, the uncertainty, the fear, the insecurity, the "uncomfortable" emotions that arose when I wasn't able to accomplish what I believed so deeply was mine to conquer— those were feelings that needed to be held within the boundaries that defined them. They did *not* need to sneak past their threshold of influence onto what was and wasn't the core of why and how I operated in any given scenario. In summary, deep beneath the surface those emotions were not a part of what defined me—but I had to *choose* to believe that and then act out of that truth.

What came next was the process of actively defining what my true purpose and core values were. This was not something that could be decided in a vacuum. I needed truth tellers speaking into my life who could highlight what was genuine and help me break away what wasn't. This will look different for everyone because your definition of community is culturally, socially, and personally influenced. For some it's blood and blood only. For others, it's your sisterhood/brotherhood, or a few close friends. It could be a church small group, a faith leader, a bonus mom/dad, or a life coach. The critical factor is these people need to KNOW you. Which also means you need to let yourself be KNOWN by them.

I recognize that we aren't all fortunate enough to have these spaces. Create what you need. You will find that there are people who are willing to declare, if they haven't already, spaces for authentic purpose finding. If you still struggle in find this space, email me: deb@embracinguncomfortable.com. Let's talk.

You guessed it: this would be uncomfortable. So I allowed my tribe in. My faith was foundational. For me, the core of my identity was then and is now being created in God's image. I had to repeat this truth in my head over and over to remind myself I was already known: "so walk in Him, having been firmly rooted and now being built up" (Col. 2:6–7). For me, the reminder that I was *already firmly rooted* before all this supposed upheaval took place was a source of comfort. Everything I was going through now was the building up part. Hard, yes, but I had the assurance of a solid foundation beneath me. I also stepped beyond my one-on-one relationship with God and let in my Dad, my circle of friends who'd known me since junior high, two individuals who had become like second parents, several fellow colleagues, and my own therapist, who all listened and offered insight into what seemed to both drive and ground me.

As a side note, while I believe the foundational work started on that frozen beach, the application continues to evolve as my circumstances change. In relocating, my tribe has evolved too. Those who know me extend a bit further and as my siblings have gotten older and wiser, I've intentionally invited them into this process.

PRACTICING THE PURPOSE

As the misleading and misguided influences were sifted out, a clearer picture of my purpose and values rose to the surface. Not surprisingly, the personal challenge to embrace uncomfortable was a constant in my life, as were relationships, my faith, being consistent and dependable, taking time to learn and grow through listening and exploring diverse perspectives, and finally making an intentional commitment to pursue those things I deemed core to my identity. So, in the end (and by "in the end" I really mean the ongoing end, because if you think I arrived at my purpose and core values mid-chapter 3, uh no. I'm just letting you know I arrived, but the ETA was a long one) I arrived at the following:

Purpose: To embrace the uncomfortable in order to fulfill the calling of community.

Values: Jesus, relationship, wisdom, authenticity, purpose*

Then came time for application. For me, community equals connection, so choosing to step into uncomfortable spaces was driven by my desire to come together, not drive apart. Here's another tangible example of what that looked like. Remember the disgruntled coffee shop lady from chapter 1? Let me tell you how the rest of that story unfolded. When the Art-of-Ordering-Tea Lady finally completed her order, I stepped to the register and

---

* The next chapter will include exercises that can help you in developing and defining your own sense of purpose and values.

turned to the woman behind me. "What were you planning to order?" Her response: "Hot chocolate," with a look of irritation. So, I placed my order and added hers to it.

Brief pause for contextual clarity: as a sucker for self-assessments, let me tell you that in addition to being an Enneagram 3, I'm also an S type on the DISC profile, and about as high a J (judging) you can score on the Myers Briggs. In other words, I am ALL ABOUT JUSTICE. I'm the person who grumbles just as loud as Disgruntled Café Lady when someone behind me on an airplane tries to disembark before me.

So, ordering for and buying this woman's drink was not what the human side of my behavior would typically choose to do. However, now I had a filter I could sift my choices through. *Values* = Jesus, relationship, wisdom, authenticity, purpose. *Purpose* = Embrace the uncomfortable in order to fulfill the calling of community. Telling this woman what's what surely wouldn't align with who I was at my core, nor would it represent my values. So, one medium hot chocolate, extra whip, to go (I wasn't going to make this last longer than it needed to) it was. What followed—her surprise, an apology for her behavior, clarity to her circumstances (she was running late for her role as classroom reader for her five-year-old grandson), and me handing her my business card.*

Do you recognize the pattern? My gut was embracing the comfort myth, bowing to the situational context around me and acting accordingly. I'm confident most of the other people present in that café wanted to tell this woman off, and I also think a gentle confrontation could have been warranted. Yet, the representation of Jesus, the pursuit of connection (community),

---

* Okay, I might have been able to see the importance of patience with this woman, but don't tell me she didn't also need some therapy to deal with her anger issues or her long-line, short-fuse issues. She never did contact me, by the way.

exercising wisdom, being true to myself, and engaging my purpose required intentionality because it was momentarily uncomfortable yet carried the enduring trait of consistency with my core identity. While I don't know the long-term outcome of that brief conversation, my hope is that the impact would give her pause to consider her behavioral influence in the future.

However, even that is something I have no control over, and if I embraced it as my motivation, I would just be back to square one, allowing circumstances and situations to define my purpose, back to the old "problem-solver identity."

IN THE WORKPLACE . . .

This may be a simple example, but I believe on a grander scale it has the ability to transform us personally, corporately, and communally. I've seen this happen in my workplace. When authenticity is one of your core values, who you are tends to seep into the places you influence and interact. In the developing stages of the counseling program I direct, our team created space to intentionally define our purpose and core values. One clear priority was partnership in community and the intentional pursuit of diversity. I give my team all the credit for collaboratively speaking into the tenet of our identity and even more so engaging in the behavior(s) that are critical to its application. Knowing that growing and nurturing a diverse team would take time and purposeful decision-making and action, we established a core value of all-encompassing humility—the commitment to establishing a posture of listening to understand and learn and verbal and non-verbal actions that aligned with such.

Let me be clear, I am by no means perfect and I make mistakes. In fact, it would probably be much easier to write a "How not to" then a "How to" in this case. However, I can say with confidence that this practice of challenging the comfort myth and willingly engaging in uncomfortable practices has created a community of unique and varied experiences, cultures, approaches to mental health and wellness that more accurately (not perfectly) reflects the body that we minister to. As a team, we each come with our own experiences and perceptions, of how we view communication, teaching, the counseling dynamic, and the intricate elements of our work relationships. It is much easier to engage in the "comfort" of behaving according to personal preferences and habitual patterns. However, that practice would be contrary to the larger purpose of partnership. So, we make the conscious choice to step into and embrace the uncomfortable. Our priority is to listen first before responding because it reflects our core value of relationship. The result has been a team, not void of conflict, but deeply connected and committed to the bond of our community and the transformation of one another and the students we in turn also partner with.

> If your community resembles you in every demographic measure, the likelihood of you living in false comfort is high.

This begs to highlight the critical value of community in your pursuit of not only embracing uncomfortable but also in the establishment of your authentic values and purpose. Pause here with me for a moment and consider your community. Whether it's two people or fifteen, if your community resembles you on every demographic measure, the likelihood of you living in false or misleading comfort is high. Why? Because you're more likely to hear what you *want* to hear and not what you *need* to hear when the collective wisdom around you resembles the same school of thought.

REHOBOAM AND THE ECHO CHAMBER

Let me give you an example. Whether you know/believe in the Bible or not, I believe the stories contained therein can provide excellent proverbial wisdom. In the Old Testament there was an appointed king of Israel, King Rehoboam, fourth on the throne and son of Solomon, who was the king best known for his wisdom (read the irony here), and grandson of King David. When Rehoboam took power following the passing of his father, Israel was still a united monarchy; however, the border cities were beginning to rebel. An appointed leader of the appropriately disgruntled Israelites came to Rehoboam and asked that he consider easing the "hard service and heavy yoke" (1 Kings 12:4) his father, King Solomon, had placed on them. At first glance, Rehoboam's next steps exemplified wisdom and prudence. He sought the counsel of the "old men" who had previously advised his father, men with more experience and broader views than the forty-one-year-old, newly appointed leader.

Unfortunately, he didn't like their perspective—serve the people and lead them with kindness. So, he reached out to a group of people who bore his likeness and probably thought more in line with his viewpoint, the guys he grew up with, his friends. Their response? Make their lives *worse*, exercise an authoritarian leadership style that shows them who's boss; if their yoke was heavy with your dad, *make it even heavier*. And Rehoboam said, "I like this idea better!" (A great example of self-fulfilling one's prophecy.) The costly outcome of his decision was that "Israel has been in rebellion against the house of David to this day" (1 Kings

12:19). Rehoboam's decision to maintain a homogenous group of people speaking into his life and advising his decisions literally led to the historical downfall of an entire nation.

What can happen when we commit to a diverse community of individuals providing wisdom and insight into the most vulnerable parts of our lives? What might be momentarily uncomfortable has the potential for long-term transformative impact. Mellody Hobson, the president and CEO of Ariel Investments and Vice Chair of the Starbucks Corporation, provides an excellent narrative of this possibility in her TED talk "Color Blind or Color Brave."[2] She tells the story of how the cure for smallpox came about. At the time, the disease was infecting millions of people across Europe, so a group of scientists came together in hopes that their collective brilliant minds could develop a cure. Each attempt was a failure until a humble local dairy farmer made a casual observation that none of his milkmaids had ever been infected by the disease. To this day, the foundational component of the smallpox vaccine is bovine-based. (In fact, the word "vaccine" is related to the Latin word for cow.)

• • •

Hobson also said this: "So I think it's time for us to be comfortable with the uncomfortable conversation about race: black, white, Asian, Hispanic, male, female, all of us, if we truly believe in equal rights and equal opportunity in America, I think we have to have real conversations about this issue." Talk about a champion for embracing uncomfortable!

While there will always be moments (some long, some short) along our journey where we stumble and veer off course, the compass of knowing the unique design we're called to pour out into the world, and knowing we do have the power to choose in the moment, and knowing the convictions that we align our lives to, will always set our paths straight again.

Now on to you—and *your* unique design.

4

THE NUTS AND BOLTS: YOUR PURPOSE, YOUR VALUES

dis·po·si·tion | \ ˈdi-spə-ˈzi-shən:
what makes you, you; your natural tendencies and where you
lean into—what your heart is inclined to pursue.

What consistently shows up in all spheres of your life that
you're drawn to, would grieve if you had to sacrifice, and lights
up your eyes when you're asked about it?

What about you?

In the first three chapters I've talked about the key elements of a universal purpose and clearly applied core values. This chapter is designed to give you the real nuts and bolts of how to start on the path of defining your own. I recognize both from my own experience and in working with others that this is a uniquely personal process and also one that will take a focused and patient commitment. Just like the patterns you've established in your life, your purpose and values are not going to present themselves overnight. However, launching into uncomfortable spaces necessitates knowing who you are. It's the critical first step in providing a solid foundation for discernment when faced with the daily choices of life.

I was able to do that when I had that time at the beach. I recognize the advantage this brought me that many others may never have at their disposal. However, know that if your current circumstances don't allow for you to experience an extended period of time in a distraction-free zone, this won't preclude you from engaging in this exercise.

First, focus on what you do have—not on what you don't. Consciously reorient your thinking to recognize that every decision you make, from the smallest to the largest, involves a loss. Then ask yourself, "What can I do right now?"

Creating uninterrupted space in your life may necessitate creativity and sacrifice—but even a few daily minutes can still move you toward your goal. If you have to sit in the parked car in your garage so your toddler won't find you, stay at work for an additional twenty minutes past closing time to generate the quiet solitude that won't present itself on your long commute home, or sacrifice time out with friends for a commitment-free month of Saturdays at home, know that IT WILL BE WORTH IT. Why? Because you are worth it. My best friend, who teaches seventh grade (literally the definition of *bless your heart*), finds space to pause and adjust her decision to reflect her values by hiding in the classroom closet for a few minutes. She also told

The awesome thing about defining your values is you really can't fail at this process.

me she has a habit of stealing away to "take a shower" and just sitting on the bathroom floor to reflect while the water runs. Environmentally questionable, yes, but for her, a distraction-free ten minutes or so!

The other point I want to emphasize is that this process *does not have to be perfect.* The goal is not to wait until you've solidified your values and tattooed them permanently on your arm. This is going to be a fluid process, and if you're a check-the-box-on-your-to-do-list kind of person, well, you get to step into the process of embracing uncomfortable right now! The awesome thing about defining our values is you really can't fail at this process. In my experience, people don't put down things that *aren't* important to them. It's more about finding those values that represent the greatest importance and cover a broad range of experiences—the larger umbrella of value categories, if you will. So, before we move on, say this out loud: "I'm committed to this process and I won't let perfection stand in my way."

WHAT IS MOST IMPORTANT IN MY LIFE?

Since this is a deeply personal experience, my outline here is meant to be loosely followed as more of a guide and less a prescription. What worked for me may not work for you, but the goal is to take the examples here and craft them to your personality and situation. I am not the expert on you (I'm barely the expert on me). That being said, what was helpful for me as a starting point was to simply write down all the people, places, objects, and memories that flashed across my mind when I considered the question, "What is most important in my life both in the present and in the past?" You might conjure up a list a mile long or you might write down five things and call it a day. Again, either one is okay! I also want to note that you might be one of those people who become easily frustrated with this activity because you struggle to remember what happened yesterday. That's also okay! I've got some suggestions for you in just a bit—keep reading!

Depending on how you approach this task, make sure you devote an intentional period of time to really consider what you value most. If you're able to sneak away for this activity and have ample time for concentrated self-reflection, take a day (at least!) to flush this list out. If you're working through this activity between the demands of your daily life, set an alarm on your smartphone labeled "values" and give yourself five minutes to review this question daily over a week or two.

As your list begins to develop, one important practice is to commit to non-judgment and *no interpreting* at this point. What I mean by non-judgment is avoiding (or challenging if avoidance fails) statements such as "my values *should* include this" or allowing yourself to believe that certain values are better or more important than others. Just like trying to match your looks to the latest "IT" celebrity, the comparison game can heap feelings of inadequacy and disappointment on this process. It can also be hard to look back on our lives and not see our memories through the context of our present. Note that the values we *truly* align with are more static, more unchanging, across our lifetime. Meaning, they were probably present when you were young without you consciously recognizing them. Unless you are intentionally trying to project them onto the past (likely as a result of the comparison game), chances are they were already there to begin with.

Let me pause here and provide a bit of insight on tapping into memories. As I mentioned, for some it can be very challenging. We're each created on a spectrum of recollection ability. If you struggle with surfacing memories of the past, consider reaching out to family, "family," or friends that were a part of your life at that time. Their narratives can also provide valuable insight into the world of your values and purpose. Also, please know that if you *still* struggle to identify specific memories, this doesn't preclude you from engaging in this exercise. Even the vaguest representation of a memory (the smile on someone's face, the feeling you experienced, the scenery) can represent the beginnings of a value. Sometimes providing a structure around memory reflection can be helpful. Consider constructing a timeline of memories and seeing what bubbles to the surface. Divide your life into a timeline and see what comes up from ages zero to six, seven to twelve, thirteen to eighteen, nineteen to thirty . . . and so on. Any memory that comes to mind can go on the list. We'll address how they represent values in a moment.

I also want to intentionally acknowledge that for many, the memories of the past can carry dark and painful reminders of trauma or loss. Again, this exercise is designed to work *with* you not against you. If sitting with the experiences of your childhood or even more recent times is not safe, please do not go there or consider doing so in the presence of a safe person who can provide comfort in the form of listening and empathic validation.

It's also important to note that all memories will not be positive memories and they don't have to be. The absence of desires can also lend clarity to the things most important to us. If you longed for deep, enduring relationships as a child or young adult but seemed to only encounter loneliness or superficial surface connections, this could highlight a value of relationship or intimacy.

To give you some ideas, here's a peek at some of the items on my list:

- Dad
- Sister
- Brother
- Bible
- Church
- Backpacking through Europe after high school with Sarah
- Getting my PhD
- Smartphone/calendar
- Letters from my birth mom
- My closest group of girlfriends
- My journals and scrapbooks
- The comfort of home
- Youth group
- Spiritual direction
- Giving the eulogy at my mom's funeral
- Counseling clients

- Walking to "the store" and selling ice cream out of my grandparent's house with my cousins in Seibert, CO
- The day my sister was born
- The day my parents brought my brother home from Lebanon
- Helping a teacher in high school who went through a tragic loss
- Playing in the dirt mound with my dad near my childhood home in Massachusetts
- My tattered copy of *Alexander and the Terrible, Horrible, No Good, Very Bad Day*
- My dog
- Sneaking into award shows

- Going to school on the bus with my mom when she was a teacher
- Moving high schools and running for student council
- Watching my nephews come into the world
- Reading books in coffee shops and cars
- Defending my dissertation
- Paul and Becky
- Getting baptized
- Working on the farm with my grandparents
- My best friend
- Personal therapy
- The beach house in Virginia

Again, this is just a snippet of my list. Just like for you, my list is deeply personal and there are items on it that are between me and God or me and my closest inner circle of people.

WHAT DOES IT MEAN?

Once your ideas start to dwindle, move on to the next goal, to consider what these memories really mean for you. For example, let me unpack the memory of switching high schools and running for student council. Remember that one of the greatest fears I've wrestled with throughout my life is that of *belonging*. I was painfully shy as a child. I was a pastor's kid for most of my childhood years, and every picture I have with my parents at church shows me peeking out from the folds of my mother's dress with a barely-there smile and deer-in-the-headlights eyes. To that end, I worked to situate myself in positions of fitting in, because standing out in any way was terrifying. I could (and still can) be a chameleon to anyone who doesn't know me well. I tried throughout my elementary and high school years to copy whatever was popular. If reading was the thing, I read every book assigned so if I was called on in class, I could quickly answer a question and the attention would be diverted to someone else. If some new game at recess was all the rage, I was determined to be the best and be the first (or at least not the last!) picked in that horrible "team captain" style way of determining who was "it" and who clearly wasn't.

Yet the memory of running for student council didn't align with memories of wanting to blend into the shadows. This memory was of wanting to challenge myself to step out and pursue a leadership opportunity. Once you're labeled in school, it's really difficult to shake that baked-in perception of you as (insert stereotype here). And for someone who wanted to *fit in*, challenging the label wasn't easy to do. However, here was a new opportunity, new school, new friends, new Deb. Running for student council in the context of a new community that didn't know my past history of quiet conformity was the circumstance I needed to challenge my own growth and embrace something uncomfortable. Reflecting on that experience brought an intense recollection of feeling the anxiety of wanting to blend into the day-to-day, but also feeling the excitement and urge to get involved as a leader and influencer. Not typically something you can do from the safety net of anonymity.

Once you've captured, as much as possible, the meaning behind each item on your list, take a step back and consider things from a 30,000-foot view. As you take time to develop a picture of some of your most impactful experiences, consider what's floated to the surface as a box full of puzzle pieces ready to be connected together. I'm a nerd for puzzles and typically approach the task of piecing one together by first sorting out the themes that initially catch my eye. Edge pieces group together, as do certain colors and shapes. Memories and the values they represent can be grouped together to illustrate repeating themes in your life.

Now consider context: Are your values applied consistently across different settings? Too often we choose to base our values on what seems appropriate at the time, to the situation, the people we're with, and so on. You might call it a situation-ethics frame of reference instead of an internally motivated, consistent application of what is most important to us. If your values are relative instead of absolute, you're more likely to engage in reactive versus intentional behavior, finding yourself in the discomfort zone. Who you are at home, who you are at work, who you are with your siblings or your small group: those "selves" should line up with relative consistency.

For me, the more reflection I put into the memory of running for student council the more I saw how it captured the importance of growth in my life, much like personal therapy and spiritual direction. Yet I also saw growth as something that happens outside of the time and energy we might put into it. People, circumstances, change all ignite growth in our life. I began to see a connection between those things and another item on my list—reading books in coffee shops and cars (that I'm riding in). I will quickly take an opportunity to read on any and every occasion. The words of my mom are still so vivid in my head of summer car trips to national landmarks: "Deborah, put your book down and look outside!" To this day, a book will always serve to soothe my restless mind and quench my thirst for knowledge from diverse sources of experience. Reading books and the desire for growth helped clarify my pursuit of wisdom (and the tendency toward self-criticism when my perception suggests I've failed in applying this value in a particular situation).

Similarly, when I considered the impact of backpacking through Europe at eighteen (parents, what were you thinking?), sneaking into awards shows, and even running for student council, while the sense of adventure was evident in those experiences, the significant outcome for me was putting my money where my mouth was, saying I could do scary, unknown things and then actually doing them. This triggered me to think how, when I teach a class, equip a client, coach a group (write a book) on a topic that I was not consistently practicing in my own life, I am often left squirming.

THE ELIMINATION ROUND

As you can see, these exercises can lead to layer upon layer of insight. And once you've reflected on the meaning of your memories, now it's time to step into the discomfort of this exercise. Values are intrinsically intertwined with emotion. If you glance at your list and one item on there doesn't evoke a strong sense of nostalgia, elation, joy, pain, contentment, or peace, it probably doesn't belong on the list. You'll see why as we move on to the elimination round. No matter how often I coach people through this activity, it always makes them squirm. It did for me and it likely will for you. Just embrace it and let's go!

Start by crossing five items off your list. Here's the kicker: removing those items means, *metaphorically*, they never existed in your life—the memory, the person, the object, the place. You didn't have it, know them, own it, or go there ... ever. As I said, this is going to be **uncomfortable**. That's exactly the point. Every day we make decisions that conflict with and contradict our values. Push through the discomfort of this and take whatever time necessary to complete the task. Getting to your core values doesn't mean that other things aren't important to you. But it does mean that what you ultimately end up with would drastically alter who you are if it ceased to be a part of your daily decisions and interactions.

Take your time with this part of the exercise. Allow yourself to sit with the discomfort as long as you can. Our emotions will always influence the way we view and interpret things. Engaging your community as you explore what drives you is critical. Ask a friend to meet you for coffee and process through the experience. Talk to your spouse about it. Make a second appointment with your therapist this week. Seek out a pastor, small group leader, or a wise colleague, professor, mentor, or boss who can offer perspective. If you really want to get to the heart of who you are, you have to be willing to get vulnerable. Even if you don't agree with what is shared, make a commitment now that you'll be willing to press against the discomfort of certain emotions and stay reflective in this process. This will enhance your ability to cast out feedback that is really inaccurate but also keep that which might not be easy to receive but does adequately depict some of your shadow sides. Ultimately, through individuals and corporate reflection, the goal is to whittle the list down to a manageable number of items (think a minimum of five and no more than ten).

CAPTURING THE "WHY"

With the remaining items, the goal is to revisit *themes*. Ultimately, you want to capture what each piece of your list represents for you—the *why* behind its importance. If you're one of those individuals who simply *couldn't* cut the list to size, what is remaining and where might the similarities lie? On my list were a lot of important people in my life. I honestly cannot imagine life without any one of them. Funny enough, the object *Alexander and the Terrible, Horrible, No Good, Very Bad Day* represented *broken relationships*. Alexander, the poor kid, is left out all day long. He's looked over in the carpool ride, told by his best friend he's been replaced, and his mom forgets his dessert, and then he's the scapegoat for his brothers' bad behavior. Every time my mom or dad read me that book at bedtime, I remember wanting to crawl into the story and just give Alexander a hug!

Look for the deeper meaning in the items on your list. A warm fuzzy feeling is just the beginning. Grouping together my family, friends, church community, and yes, Alexander and his terrible day, revealed that relationships are key to my life. I readily saw this on my list but that opened the door to see how I often project this value onto others as well. When people share with me their hurts or struggles, I often view them through the lens of broken community (just like I did with good ol' Alex). When my relationships are not functioning well, I can easily become fixated on what I need to do to solve the problem. This illustrates another way to sift out a core value. Identifying what is most important to us can happen when we see or experience that value tangibly playing out but also when we encounter its absence and the resulting consequences in our lives.

Use the boxes below to list the items that remained as you powered through the discomfort of elimination. Again, try to group what remained according to categories and then sit with the outcome for at least a day or so, take longer if you need to and also engage others in their feedback.

CATEGORY

CATEGORY

CATEGORY

CATEGORY

CATEGORY

After you've mulled your categories and the values within each, see if one or two rises to the top as representing the meaning of that category. If you need help with value words, check out the list at the end of this chapter.

> Don't look for the "right" answer, look for the "you" answer.

Now that you've established a basic understanding of what you lean toward values-wise, it can be helpful to place your conclusions in context. Take your self-reflection a bit further by responding thoughtfully to the following questions. Much like the Values exercise, this is best done in multiple stages. Consider whatever comes to mind first and write it down. Then sit with the answers for a while (a few hours, days, a week—again, the idea is whatever works best for you). Try to eliminate any pressure that you're looking for the *right* answer and instead shift your perspective to looking for the *you* answer. Once you feel at least somewhat confident in your answers, pause and consider whether or not your values are revealed in your answers. If yes, consider yourself on the right track! If no, what is misaligned? Your values or your actions?

1. If I could have anything in the world, what would it be?
2. When I am alone, what do I think about most?
3. How do I spend my discretionary funds? Is my home a place to live or a showplace?
4. How do I spend my leisure time?
5. Who do I pick for my friends?
6. Who are the three people I most admire? Why?
7. What kinds of things do I laugh at?

If your responses to the above questions or the values exercise as a whole has left you feeling frustrated or defensive, commit to the discomfort of taking responsibility and avoid blaming others or making excuses for where you are instead of where you want to be. Avoidance might seem easier now and it's always less intimidating than making changes, but it's the trade-off of short-term comfort for long-term distress.

PURPOSE: NOT WHAT YOU DO, BUT WHO YOU ARE

After you've taken time to consider your core values, you can transition to clarifying your essential purpose. But be careful with this. I did a simple web search on "how to define your purpose" and there were over 300 million results! While I didn't have the time to read *every* listed outcome, even just clicking on the hits in the first page revealed the overwhelming focus of purpose being connected to production and vocation. No wonder people tightly hinge themselves to what they do. Purpose goes so far beyond that! It needs to include who we are and who we are becoming. Production is a product of vocation and it shifts and changes at various points in our lifetime. The consequence of placing purpose in a limiting box means the minute your circumstances don't align with your identified purpose, you're left feeling lost and often insignificant. Purpose needs to cover the near-totality of our daily choices and interactions. So the next important step is to shift your perspective on purpose from *what you do* to *who you are*.

Once you've clarified this, you can shift your statement to action words. I'll use my purpose as an example:

Who I am: I am someone who embraces uncomfortable because I am someone who highly values community.

What I do: I embrace the uncomfortable in order to fulfill the calling of community.

Much like discerning your values, clarifying your purpose will take intentional reflection and patience. A great first step is taking time to consider the stories you like to tell about the experiences in your life. Again, consider these narratives without judgment and don't be too quick to dismiss experiences you initially interpret as having nothing to do with your purpose. I'll give you an example.

A favorite story I love to tell others is how I made a hobby out of sneaking into awards shows while I was in grad school.* Don't ask me what sparked the idea, but I recruited an equally brave friend and we persuaded ourselves that throwing on old bridesmaid dresses and plastering "party" makeup all over our faces would convince the Secret Service–level security detail for "Hollywood's biggest nights!" that we belonged among the rich and famous. After all, I *did* have some experience in the wrangling of celebrities. Surely I could now act like one. In what I can only describe as some cosmic aligning of the *stars*, in one thrilling moment of pure adrenaline, I grabbed my friend's hand, put on an air of A-list importance, and thrust us through a crowd of photographers, right past security and into the fabulous spotlight of stardom. It was exhilarating, uncomfortable, and I loved it.

Now, clearly my purpose doesn't include the word *trespassing*, but I've always been drawn to activities, situations, and relationships that make me a little uncomfortable. In the moment, it might not be pleasant but the aftermath of the experience, if accurately aligned with my purpose and values, always brings a sense

---

* Seven failed attempts on the comprehensive exam and borderline felony behavior—
  I'm the poster child for a successful doctoral student.

of fulfillment and satisfaction. For you it might well be something else. But be alert to those occasions.

I believe one of the biggest mistakes we've made with purpose is connecting it with passion. Now, don't get me wrong, I think purpose can ignite feelings of passion. I have had some amazing experiences where I'm fully engaged in my sweet spot and experiencing that ignition that comes from being fully immersed in who you were designed to be. However, I don't think I'm built to experience full passion at all times. That sounds exhausting! In fact, walk with me as I diverge from the trail a bit. This is where we get all twisted up when it comes to emotion. We pursue this idea that our true goal, where we really want to arrive at, is intensely positive emotions at all times (and nothing *un*pleasant). Well, that's impossible and only sets us up for failure. We're not wired to experience an intensity of emotion, be it anxiety, depression, excitement, or passion, for an extended period of time. We're designed to return to a baseline of peace. So, I would argue that peace and contentment are the true markers of being aligned with your purpose. Similarly, their antonyms, feeling unsettled and disappointed (otherwise known as discomfort—see how I did that), can actually provide great insight into those areas where we're functioning outside purpose.

Now comes the hard part—making some changes and establishing new priorities. Remember, this is going to take sacrifice. If you're willing to embrace that reality now, you can begin to focus on pursuing the greater gain while avoiding the greater loss. Choosing to live according to our values and purpose is a choice of allowing our core principles to address the circumstances that are uniquely ours. The willingness to embrace the brief experience of uncomfortable produces the outcome of decision-making based on perception, discernment, clear thinking, and intentionality—but we have to make space in our lives to see and act on the steps necessary to move us in that direction.

VALUES EVALUATION

I surveyed a number of colleagues, professionals, friends, and family to create the list of values below. You can also search the internet for a never-ending list of values. Just beware of analysis paralysis. Read over the words and put a check mark next to every value that resonates with you, or add your own in the fill-in-the-blank spots. You're not chiseling your values into stone here, so don't worry if you're not sure about one initially or if you change your mind later on. The goal is to compare this list with the list of people, objects, memories, and places you identified above. Then, ask yourself if these values represent something you refuse to compromise on (think, "touch it and I'll punch you." Or, less violently, "this feels like something that's just in my blood").

_____ Accountability	_____ Family
_____ Active empathy	_____ Fearlessness
_____ Adventure	_____ Friendship
_____ Authenticity	_____ Freedom
_____ Autonomy	_____ Fun
_____ Balance	_____ Generosity
_____ Beauty	_____ Genuineness
_____ Boundaries	_____ Goodness
_____ Challenge	_____ Gratitude
_____ Collaboration	_____ Growth
_____ Compassion	_____ Happiness
_____ Competition	_____ Health
_____ Community	_____ Honesty
_____ Congruence	_____ Hospitality
_____ Connection	_____ Humanity
_____ Contribution	_____ Humility
_____ Courage	_____ Humor
_____ Creativity	_____ Inclusion
_____ Culture	_____ Independence
_____ Curiosity	_____ Influence
_____ Dependability	_____ Ingenuity
_____ Determination	_____ Integrity
_____ Development	_____ Joy
_____ Discipline	_____ Justice
_____ Excellence	_____ Kindness
_____ Efficiency	_____ Leadership
_____ Equality	_____ Loyalty
_____ Excellence	_____ Love
_____ Expression	_____ Organization
_____ Faith	_____ Passion
_____ Faithfulness	_____ Patience

_____Peace   _____Transparency

_____Perseverance _____Truth

_____Positivity   _____Vulnerability

_____Purpose   _____Wholeness

_____Respect   _____Wisdom

_____Safety   _____Work

_____Self-actualization _____ _____

_____Service   _____ _____

_____Sincerity   _____ _____

_____Time   _____ _____

_____Tradition   _____ _____

THE DISCIPLINED PURSUIT OF PAUSING IN A WORLD FULL OF "GO"

pur·suit | \ pər-ˈsüt of the \ ˈpˈz:
the intentional practice of halting our habitual patterns
and unconscious behaviors to reevaluate our direction
and reorient our compass.

*Where do you need to add the daily discipline of
pausing to your life in order to fully step into the
practice of embracing uncomfortable?*

My dad recently returned for another Chicago visit and promptly shared how excited he was to walk the city with me again. Every morning we got ready and headed out on the familiar route to work, watching the city wake up to the eager commute of pedestrians heading to their various offices and listening to harried drivers navigating their cars through growing traffic jams in order to transport their passengers across town. My dad and I love to chat, and there's no shortage of topics we're able to cover. So, on a forty-minute walk we can easily become distracted with the details of whatever conversation we're engrossed in.

I noticed a problem with that this year. I've been walking for a while now and I'm familiar with the unspoken "road rules" of pedestrian transportation; my dad, a Chicago visitor, is not. So, here's what would happen as we closed in on a busy intersection. I would slow down and observe traffic: Are there cars coming, is the light green, will that pigeon make it? My dad, chit-chatting away, would simply follow the person in front of him. Now, Chicago walkers will cross the street without a care in the world and little to no regard for oncoming traffic. Needless to say, on more than one occasion I found myself frantically throwing my arms out to stop my dad from taking a direct hit from a passing car. That's a game of Frogger you aren't going to win, Dad. To be fair, I am my father's daughter, so I'm not claiming to follow all of the rules of the road, just stating that I'll bend the rules for efficiency as long as it doesn't result in me becoming a pancake. How do I prevent that from happening? Unlike my dad, who simply forged ahead, when we approached an intersection I paused and observed what was happening.

Unfortunately, I don't always put this practice into place in other areas of my life. It's too easy to fall into the habitual pattern of daily decisions that keep us moving forward until we come face to face with a semi-truck. It wasn't until a former assistant of mine did something so simple yet so profound that I realized how critical the discipline of pausing is in the everyday navigation of our choices and pursuits. A few years ago, I opened my computer to check my schedule and noticed something blocked off on the calendar that I didn't recognize and hadn't scheduled: "Jesus and emails—1 hour—repeated daily." Barb had recognized the unsustainable pace I was moving at and the resulting details that were slipping through my cracks, so she nudged me in a direction that shifted me away from routine and toward contemplation. What started off as "Jesus and emails" has now become the necessary disciplined pursuit of pause that cuts across all intersections of my life.

Now is the time in the book where we're going to put the art of embracing uncomfortable into practice. Sorry to disappoint any lingering expectations that there might still be a way to pursue easy gains for an easy life. If you aren't willing to get uncomfortable yet, even in the slightest, there's really no point in reading any further because this is where we start to get into the nitty-gritty. I've given you the what—now it's time for the how. And the how is hard. However, remember that you're not alone in this! Know when it starts to feel hard, that's when you know it's working. The how means setting boundaries and taking some hits. There will be loss, but the gains will be tremendous if you're willing to patiently wade through the process. If you're still with me, let's take that first step.

NO!

The first task of embracing uncomfortable is the purposeful choice of stepping into the discomfort of saying no regardless of the consequence. There is little hope of achieving the remaining elements of radical transformation without the discipline of pausing. This needs to be our life strategy.

When I pitched *Embracing Uncomfortable* to my publisher, I honestly had no idea what I was doing. I was walking to the meeting one morning and sending up a prayer of panic when it occurred to me (thank You, God!)—make them uncomfortable!

It was either genius or overwhelmingly naïve, but thankfully it worked (you're reading the book aren't you?). I asked the players in the room to pull out a piece of paper and write down one thing truly meaningful in their life they had been wanting to change but had so far really struggled with. Once that was accomplished, I asked them to write down all the things preventing them from making the change. Next—cross out anything on that list that was an impossibility, but I wouldn't let them toss out "time." Talk about squirming! I received plenty of pushback. And most of us tend to think like this: adding time to our life would be wonderful, but it's absolutely impossible.

Why does saying "no" scare us half to death, especially when the list of things we're sacrificing to our perceived lack of time are often valuable, important, and sometimes even life-saving?

I would argue that the reason we keep saying yes instead of no is because we've unconsciously placed our values in the hands of others. We give them (spouse, boss, parent, mom's group member, neighbor, social media follower) the power to measure us by what we accomplish and achieve on *their* scale and not our own. I call the motivation behind these yeses the "I-don't-want-tos" of life.

I don't want to fail.

I don't want to miss out.

I don't want to disappoint.

I don't want to be seen as less than.

I don't want to be left in the dust.

I don't want to _____.

The irony is, in all our efforts to avoid the "I-don't-want-tos," I bet you could *pause* here (see how I did that) and name multiple times in the last week, maybe even the last day, where you experienced or saw yourself as failing, missing out, disappointing, or not measuring up. The "I-don't-want-tos" have the system rigged! They win no matter what! Until now.

When we practice the discipline of pausing, it's like putting on a new pair of glasses when you've been walking around with an outdated prescription for far too long. It shifts everything around you and consequently everything in you into perspective. Yet, you'll also never get into the habit of disciplined pausing without shifting your perspective—it's an evil "chicken or the egg" situation. Which comes first? Sometimes it depends on how hungry you are.

LOSS: INEVITABLE, NOT AVOIDABLE

Let's start with this reality: every decision you make, from the smallest to the largest, involves a loss. I've mentioned this a few times up to this point, but it's worth repeating because it is critical to the success of embracing uncomfortable and choosing to move in alignment with your values and purpose. The loss might be big or tiny, but the loss is always present. We tend to make decisions based on the gains, not the losses. It's why we say yes. Let's go back to our list from above and plug in the "gains."

If I say yes to this, I'll gain:

Success

Inclusion

Approval

Adequacy

We might think we're gaining something in our decisions, but at what cost? Oftentimes the answer to that question carries a much greater loss than the gains we're pursuing. Think about it. If I spend more time at work accomplishing tasks, making everyone happy, and getting every last item on my to-do list done, I may have gained success, but I've lost quality connection to the key relationships in my life. If I put another activity on my kids' social schedule to show how accomplished my family is, keep up with the Joneses, and make sure my child doesn't feel left out, I may have gained approval, but I've lost out on quality time with my family and quite possibly for myself. When I conform to the style/behavior/expectation of the media and popular culture, I may have gained inclusion, but I've lost my unique identity. Don't fool yourself into thinking loss is avoidable—challenge yourself to embrace that loss is inevitable.

When we consider the truth that's there's always a loss and we willingly shift to consider the greater loss we want to avoid, we all of a sudden open ourselves up to the option of pursuing choices that align more with our values and less with others' expectations. Yes, this is uncomfortable, but only for a season.

Okay, let's pause here for a moment. I want to consider how this mindset is different from those of you who might be thinking right now, "But Dr. Deb, you don't understand, my life is made up of losses. I'm constantly losing and never gaining. Loss is inevitable in my life. When do the gains kick in?" Like all good decision-making, this requires balance. Just like we can focus too much on the gains in life, we can also get trapped in fixating on our losses. Losses are painful, traumatizing, overwhelming, suffocating, and yes, inevitable. Don't think for one minute I'm asking you to minimize or invalidate your losses. Loss requires mourning. I could write an entire book on the lost art of lamentation, but in this brief space hear that I'm advocating for your need to grieve the losses in your life that have left unavoidable

Dopamine is like the body's natural shiny gold star.

scars on your heart. Then, when you're ready or when you're willing (these two don't always line up, unfortunately), step into the
choices you do have power over and consider the loss you want to
avoid for the gain you want to embrace.

YOUR BRAIN ON DOPAMINE

So why can't we simply commit to this discipline and see our lives
quickly change for the better? One word. Dopamine. Dopamine
is like the body's natural shiny gold star. When you do something
that you've attached pleasure to (if you're like me, even just crossing an item off your to-do list will do it), dopamine is your reward.
It's a chemical released in the brain that actually makes you *feel*
better.[1] Worse, it causes you to crave whatever action led to the
reward again and again. Silicon Valley is *literally* designing apps
with reward schedules designed to reinforce our "clicking" behavior. As your body continues to incentivize your behavior with the
promise of more dopamine, your brain begins to create neural
pathways that trigger less and less conscious decision-making.
Think of those pathways like the gutter in a bowling lane—if your
ball ends up there it's headed in one direction only.

The good news is, we can actually change the chemical structure in our brains! When I was growing up my grandfather was a
wheat farmer. Every summer I would go with him to the farm and
help drive Big Ben (our combine) as we cultivated the ground
for sowing. Regardless of how far we were from the farmhouse,
we always ended up on the same path that led us straight home. I
remember my grandpa telling me once that it didn't matter if we
drove over that path with Big Ben; the ground had been trampled
down for so many years that the actual chemistry of the soil had
changed. It wouldn't be conducive to sowing or growth without

several years of revitalizing to restore the soil. While his message was intended to comfort me about my fear of getting lost on the expansive plains of the farm, my takeaway was that forging new pathways was always possible but not always easy or immediate.

We've all created habitual pathways in our brain from the action/reward principle. The key to forging new pathways is commitment and persistence. This means the discipline of pausing is going to take more than a simple decision. It's going to require intentionality over and over again, along with self-grace to recognize you're going to make mistakes along the way. Pause here and reread that last sentence. Do it again and do so at a slower pace. Remember that it takes commitment and persistence. Good job. Now let's continue. I can tell you from experience this is where most of us get stuck. If we're wired for reward, our instinctual response when we don't receive one is "this isn't working." Game over. Your frog just got plowed by a semi-truck.

> If we're wired for reward, our instinctual response when we don't receive one is "This isn't working."

I'm going to say it over and over again from this point on: every outcome suggested in this book is a moot point if you're unwilling to engage in the discipline of pausing. Without pausing there's no perspective, and without perspective we fall back into the trap of comfort. Trust me, no one instinctively chooses uncomfortable things. I once read that our brain reacts to choices like free-flowing water. What is the option with the least resistance and the greatest incentive?[2] To fully engage in this practice, we need to purposefully *choose* the discomfort of saying no to some things and yes to others.

"No." Why does it spark such cringeworthy reactions in us? For someone like me, sometimes the very thought of uttering the word no evokes the same effect as a 350-foot roller coaster drop. I fear disappointing others, believing they'll think less of me, or that I'll miss out on something really great. "No" meant I would cause others to experience disapproval or rejection; therefore, it was too hard to say. I was stuck thinking I needed the word "No" to mean something different in my life in order to put it into practice. But the definition of no is never going to change. Also, shocker, I'm human and so are the people around me and that means even in my best intentions I'm going to disappoint someone (heck, you might be reading this book and I'm letting you down). If avoiding "no" to enhance the pleasure of others is my motivation in life, I might as well add the weighted bricks of bitterness, anger, and resentment to my life luggage as I attempt to dodge the semi truck. If we go back to the principle of all decisions involving loss in the consideration of a "no" response, those outcomes might be reality. However, did I stop to consider what I might lose in the process of saying a hastily decided yes?

When was the last time you intentionally said no to something you *really* wanted to do? If you're anything like me, the answer didn't readily come to mind, or perhaps the answer didn't emerge at all. We've become a "yes" society. We hastily make commitments and decisions, perhaps because we've become conditioned to respond without thinking in a society where the answers are always right at our fingertips. Or we're afraid; afraid of judgment, disappointing others, or simply missing out (Fear of Missing Out, or **FOMO,** is literally in the Oxford Dictionary now). We can't even say "no" to the next episode of that new TV show we're infatuated with. "Binge-watching" is another vocabulary word making its way into the regular rotation of things we communicate with our friends over lunch.

Unfortunately, the consequence of constant "yes" can be the loss of integrity and congruence with our values, greater feelings of dissatisfaction, heightened stress, failure to fulfill our purpose, and the increased likelihood of disappointing ourselves and others. In the practice of saying "yes," we've lost the purpose of saying "no."

I see this in the people I work with all the time (students, staff, clients . . . myself). We have this mentality of "one more thing will get me there." Fill in the blank for whatever your "there" is—a new relationship, a step up the corporate ladder, an advanced income level, greater significance. The real problem lies in the fact that we don't stop and think about what the real goal of our yes is. When we have not intentionally defined our values, purpose, or the legacy we hope to live by, a simple yes can spiral into a set of decisions that fall in stark contrast to those things most important to us.

> We have this mentality of "one more thing will get me there."

Of course, the ultimate irony is that answering these questions takes the discipline of saying "no" in order to create the time and space to reflect and explore and respond. I don't want to sidestep the reality that nos are hard. It's no fun to feel like you've disappointed someone you genuinely care about. It isn't pleasant to admit that maybe you *can't* do it all, contrary to your carefully cultivated image (see "Failure" a few chapters back). "Nos" are usually way more uncomfortable initially; but the keyword here is *initially*. It's our over-committed, inconsistent-with-my-values yeses that bring much more discomfort in the long run.

PRACTICING THE PAUSE

So how do we increase our nos in order to enhance our yeses and bring them in line with what is most important to the core of our purpose? I bet you can guess (if you aren't reading this book while binge-watching your favorite show) . . .

We practice the art of the pause.

A pause, an actual stopping, creates space for perspective. Sometimes our pause just needs to last a few seconds, a deep breath or two that grounds us to how we are feeling in the moment and gives clarity to a quick decision because the commitment is minimal or the action is familiar (is it reasonable to be a few minutes late to my meeting in order to wrap up this conversation? Is it consistent with the values I represent to others?). For other responses we may need more time—hours, possibly days. This tends to be the harder choice for most because it carries the greater likelihood of disappointing others or even ourselves. In order to prepare for this possibility, create communication strategies ahead of time. Here's an example: "That's a great question/request. Let me think about it for a few hours/days and I'll get back to you by *this* time with a decision." Our answers don't have to be complicated and they don't have to include all the details.

In his book *Essentialism: The Disciplined Pursuit of Less,*[3] author Greg McKeown argues that by taking the time to purposefully choose those things that are most important to us, we live a life of "design" rather than "default." He calls this practice "clarifying your essential intent." Simply put, we discipline ourselves to create the space necessary to make choices consistent with our values and purpose. It's hard and intentional work and it won't happen without first exercising some uncomfortable nos in order to ensure we're saying the right yeses.

Another way of putting it: practicing the discipline of pausing means we need to become less reactive and more purposeful. We need to embrace the mindset of intentionality and commit to not letting go. We need to stop allowing ourselves to engage in mindless activities without taking the time to consider the impact such choices are having on our well-being (or those around us)—mentally, physically, emotionally, and spiritually. Let's be honest, most of us are consistently making too many choices without the discipline of intentionality. We're simply reacting. Must do. Must respond. Must meet the deadline no matter the cost. Must match up. Must be relevant. The list goes on. When working with clients, without fail, reactivity is associated with defensiveness or justification (one could easily argue those two go hand-in-hand). When was the last time you made a healthy decision, or even a clarified one, in the throes of a defensive response?

When was the last time you made a healthy decision in the midst of a defensive response?

But what does this actually look like? How do you pause at work, school, driving with your spouse, talking to your kid? Do you remove yourself from a room for a few seconds, rock yourself in a corner, run to your car for a quick Skype session with your therapist? This is going to look different for everyone and every situation. What *is* going to be the same is that true intentionality requires patience. It necessitates stopping the chaos (or stepping out of the routine) momentarily and developing awareness of our thoughts, actions, feelings, and attitudes. Simply put, it means owning what we say and what we do, which requires *knowing* what we say and do!

Practicing the discipline of pausing—embracing intentionality —means:

1. Identifying and remaining true to our convictions, even in the face of temptation
2. Acknowledging the role and contribution of others
3. Choosing our words carefully
4. Creating a culture of accountability
5. Demonstrating respect (self and others)
6. Practicing consistency

Another simple strategy for creating space to pause: put it on your calendar. Again, this might work for some and not as much for others, but it may be worth a try! This is what Barb did for me and what I continue to put into practice to this day. She started recognizing a pattern in my life that needed changing. If there was a spot open on my calendar when someone was requesting time in my schedule, I would be quick to respond with a yes. So, she went through my weeks and put those strategically placed "Jesus and emails" appointments in each day. Whether I needed a break, a catch-up, or a moment of solitude, that time created intentional space in my day that disciplined me to pause and consider where I was at, how I was doing, and where I needed to go.

Practicing the pause reminds me of why the remote control was created. We literally have the power to pause a show in order to take a bathroom break, fill up on snacks, answer a text, hit send on that email still sitting in the chasm of your draft box. We can't really pause life, but we can pause ourselves. I can't think of a space we take up that isn't managed by time or scheduled agendas. Think about it. We're always being ushered (like herds) into one place and out of another. It feels like other people have a grip on the time constraints in our lives. Why do they get to call the shots? The discipline of pause is an active action that empowers you to call the shots in your own life—and now it's your turn.

How are you doing? Where do you need to go? Take a moment to pause and consider.

6

RADICAL ACCEPTANCE

rad·i·cal | \ ˈra-di-kəl ac·cep·tance | \ ik-ˈsep-tən(t)s:
taking the great steps necessary to own where you're at
regardless of season or circumstance in order to authentically
determine what you want and need to transform.

Where do you find yourself in avoidance of the real aspects of
your life, and how can you lovingly embrace where you're at in
order to process the losses and the disappointments,
and then shift the dynamics of your situation?

Year one of my postgraduate training, I was exposed to a fascinating form of treatment called Dialectical Behavior Therapy (DBT). Combining both cognitive behavioral therapeutic techniques and mindfulness and acceptance skills (part of what's known as the Third Wave of behavioral therapies), DBT challenges people to increase self-awareness of their emotions, thoughts, and behaviors, accept their current experiences, and move forward in this delicate dance of balancing validation with change.

As I began to learn and implement the skills of DBT in my work with clients, I was struck by how often individuals struggled to implement that middle step, accepting their current experiences. DBT's founder, Dr. Marsha Linehan, coined a term for this process: "radical acceptance." In her years of research with highly suicidal clients, what Dr. Linehan frequently found was that many were stuck in a thought process of denying, avoiding, or judging their current reality. Consequently, their behavior stemmed from their judgments of all-or-nothing thinking (nothing will ever change), denial of their role in the problem, or avoidance of difficult relationships, circumstances, or self-assessment due to faulty perceptions of being enslaved to their emotions. Without radical acceptance, those clients were stuck in an endless cycle of downward spirals labeled "shoulds," "what-ifs," and "if-onlys." They were simply unable to establish a genuine foundation for where they were at in life. Radical acceptance was the essential and non-negotiable key to recognizing their location, resources, and obstacles in order to then embark on an effective journey toward their authentic potential.

TRAPPED!

Let me give you an example of what radical acceptance looks like through the uncomfortable lens of my high school existence. In high school, I was the queen of odd and embarrassing experiences. My friends were always expecting me to recount some version of a bizarre incident I encountered (or initiated) over the weekend or even just in between classes before we gathered for lunch.

I served on the student newspaper with my best friend in high school, Sarah, and one time when I was two hours late for our after-school meeting, she knew a fascinating story was awaiting her. Of course there was. Wanting a snack to keep me energized for our upcoming staff meeting, I took a quick drive to Jamba Juice in my 1988 Honda Accord. With manual windows, manual drive, and manual door locks, it is still a mystery to me that the one thing *not* manual on my trusty Accord was the seatbelts. If you were born in roughly the same era as me or before and you've ever wondered why automatic seatbelts no longer exist, despite the fact that *wearing* a seatbelt is now required by law . . . here's why.

While pulling into the parking lot of the Jamba Juice, one of my Wet Seal or Charlotte Russe dangling earrings got caught on the shoulder of my blouse (yes, they were that long. . . if you weren't born in the '80s and therefore attended high school in the '90s you wouldn't understand and consequently can't judge). I reached up with my left arm to dislodge the now-painful earpiece while pulling into my parking spot, making sure to slip my hand under the seatbelt, lest I park and turn off the car only to have my automatic safety harness slide forward, causing me to pull on the earring and potentially damage my earlobe, or even worse, my business-casual blouse (I took my role as newspaper editor *very seriously*). That's when things took a turn for the worse. Placing the car in first gear, pulling the emergency brake, and turning the key to the off position, I *expected* my seatbelt to do its job, recognizing I'd arrived safely to my destination and thereby letting me free of its protective embrace. Instead, the opposite happened; the seatbelt tightened. My automatic reaction to squirm out of its grasp only served to strengthen its resolve to hold me in place even more. If only I hadn't been wearing my Swatch watch, now caught on the seatbelt and preventing me from sliding my wrist free from its awful death grip.* The more I shifted in my attempts to break free, the tighter it became.

---

* In retrospect my older self is yelling at my younger self to take the Clydesdale blinders off, use your hand, and unhinge your watch, Nancy Drew.

Now, in our present-day world of cellphones, such a predicament would easily become a "phone-a-friend" moment. Not so in 1996. I finally surrendered to my involuntary auto prison and accepted my reality that I would not be breaking out alone. What came next was the embarrassing and uncomfortable truth that I needed to roll my window down (WITH MY FOOT—because *everything* else in my car was MANUAL) and start crying for help. Needless to say, it was not exactly my proudest moment when a kind gentleman stopped, looked inquisitively into my car, did his best to stifle a laugh (he failed miserably), and reached in to press the emergency release button on the strap that was *supposed* to keep me safe but was slowly squeezing me to death.

See, it wasn't until I was willing to embrace the uncomfortable reality of my situation that I could begin taking the steps toward achieving my freedom, however embarrassing it was. This idea of radical acceptance; acknowledging our present circumstances for what they are, without judgment, minimization, or denial, is a critical foundation to any type of transformational change. In order to get where we want to go (in my case, *out of the car* and into Jamba Juice, thank you very much), we have to first truthfully recognize where we are (my current situation, stuck in my Accord, still hungry, and two hours late for my meeting). Unfortunately, we often fail to do that with honesty and grace, and we certainly fail to recognize the influence and importance of our values in these moments. Let's clarify these details using my seatbelt story.

The second that seatbelt locked me into my car, my immediate thought was "This is a simple mistake." The outcome was my squirming and the seatbelt getting tighter. Unwilling to accept my reality (denial), I squirmed and shifted and twisted even more. Consequently, the seatbelt strengthened its grasp. At this point, I surrendered my behavior but the judgments crept in. "What an idiot." "You look so dumb." "What are people going to think about you when they have to pry you out of your car with the Jaws of Life simply because you have a love-hate relationship with your seatbelt and today was the day he decided to take his revenge!"

I felt embarrassed, stupid, and helpless. Fixating on the judgments and the unpleasant emotions only furthered my entrapment. Remember, I couldn't even consider the simple task of removing my watch to possibly assist in my release to freedom! But it was only once I radically accepted I was stuck, I couldn't get out on my own, my priority was to get out, and accomplishing this task would require a call for help regardless of a change in my emotions—it was only then that I was actually able to break free. If I wanted to change my situation I was going to need to embrace uncomfortable with a large dose of humility and surrender.

> It was only when I radically accepted I was stuck and couldn't get out on my own that I was eventually able to break free.

I DIDN'T CHOOSE TO . . .

I gladly offer my self-deprecation for your reading pleasure to provide a practical example of how radical acceptance plays out in our lives. However, the truth is that we avoid radical acceptance for much more difficult things on a daily basis, often because we didn't choose our circumstances and we don't want to be there.

- I didn't choose to be single at forty-three.
- I didn't choose for my spouse to cheat on me.
- I didn't choose to lose my job.

- I didn't choose for my family member to die.
- I didn't choose to be born into a world of racism, discrimination, and hate.
- I didn't choose to be diagnosed with mental illness.
- I didn't choose for my child to struggle in school.
- I didn't choose _____.

Or sometimes we *did* make the choice(s) that brought us to our present circumstances, but we're so deeply stuck in the "if onlys," "nevers/always," "shoulds," and "should nots" that we can't get past the judgment in order to formulate a way out.

- I should never have said that to my best friend.
- If only I'd taken a chance on asking that girl out in college.
- I shouldn't still be struggling with my addiction.
- I am never going to be able to change the way I feel about this.
- I should know to listen and validate instead of question every decision my spouse makes.
- I should be able to handle this new role at work successfully.
- I shouldn't be so judgmental.
- I shouldn't react so emotionally.
- I should know better.

Radical acceptance challenges us to willingly receive our present reality despite what put us there. However, it is important to note that radical acceptance does not call us to completely dismiss the *reasons* why we are there. Instead, it dares us to embrace the present *with* the emotions brought by the journey that got us to this place, *and* the emotions accompanying us in our present circumstances, *and* the ones that join us as we move onward out of those circumstances. It is hard work and it is rarely ever a one-time deal. Radical acceptance is an ongoing process that shifts and turns with the changes in life.

When my mom passed away, I had to radically accept a new normal that now included a huge void in my life and my heart that would never be refilled. I had to radically accept she *chose* to leave this world despite all the things I

> Radical acceptance challenges us to willingly receive our present reality despite what put us there.

thought we had to offer her. I had to radically accept I felt angry, in despair, confused, lost, lonely, hopeless, afraid, inadequate, and so much more. Embracing my emotions was often the most difficult because they felt awful, and I honestly thought they would swallow me whole. Yet the opposite—denying, minimizing, judging my emotions—felt so much worse. At the very least, radical acceptance allowed me to validate where I was at.

RADICAL ACCEPTANCE IS NOT RESIGNATION

Now, here is a common mistake I see individuals make when it comes to radical acceptance. They confuse acceptance for *resignation*. They fly their white flag of surrender and succumb to a false belief that this is *always how it's going to be*. If that's what you are thinking right now as you read this chapter, let's pause for a science lesson.*

---

* My cousin Grant, who is a board-certified anesthesiologist (and the smartest person I know), verified that the description you are about to read is roughly accurate and on par with how an eight-year-old would describe the way our bodies function, so I think we're good to go. Thanks, Grant.

Our body is a complex organ with many interconnected parts working together to keep us in a state of homeostatic functioning. For example, think about your body temperature. As humans, our stable body temperature is 98.6°, any shift in that temperature and our body goes into maintenance mode to prevent something dangerous or even deadly from occurring. The same is true when it comes to our experience of emotions. Our moods have a cyclical or causal relationship with our brain. We feel an emotion, and this triggers our neurons to transfer messages between the various structures of our brain. In turn, as the structures are activated and hormones influenced, our moods are impacted. Our brain, again built to strive for homeostasis, activates various neuroprotective agents to assist in regulating our mood, preventing us from experiencing the same emotion at the same intensity indefinitely. So, the good news is you physically *can't* stay in that same awful emotional state no matter how hard you try.

Of course, there are individuals who suffer from severe mental and emotional distress for whom the regulation of emotions is a much more complicated and intense experience. In these situations, changes in mood can be so minute that it seems impossible to even recognize them. I do want to validate the frustration, anger, desperation, and anguish that can stem from struggling with such experiences. In all reality, the continuum of radical acceptance spans a chasm as big as the Grand Canyon. That's why more people take selfies in front of the Grand Canyon instead of actually hiking it. My goal is never to minimize the burden born by many from the weight of what they must radically accept. Make no mistake, this will be a challenging mission; a long, hard, frequently uphill battle with a scarcity of breaks that requires overwhelming commitment. So, it's critical to have a solid grasp of what radical acceptance is and isn't before embarking on the journey of putting it into practice.

Radical acceptance is refusing to close the sentence "it is what it is" without first adding the clarification of "in this moment."

HOW DO WE "RADICALLY ACCEPT"?

Once you've fully embraced the truth that your current circumstances are just that—the boundaries of your present reality—you are ready to begin establishing a course of action that continually guides you toward your authentic potential. So, let's take a clear and practical look at what is required for one to radically accept their current circumstances.

The first step is to describe in detail your present without judgment, minimization, or denial. For me, there were many opportunities in my twenties and thirties to radically accept my status as a single woman. As my friends married and began having kids, I was navigating graduate school, multiple jobs, and eventually supporting my sister (pseudo mom) and her new son (pseudo grandma). Time for dating was nonexistent, and frankly so was the pool of available, worthy men! Yet the loneliness of singlehood, the loss of what I had hoped and dreamed for this stage of my life, and the lies of inadequacy and hopelessness were always lurking around the corner, ready to pounce in my most vulnerable moments. Radical acceptance *did not mean* those emotions magically vanished, but it did help me set my compass to an accurate true north because I was able to correctly establish the direction I was coming from—which was this:

- I was at present single without a proper relationship prospect in my current circles of engagement (note what's missing—judgmental descriptors such as "failure," "unworthy," "ugly," "uninteresting").

- I was committed to my professional development in my doctoral program and later as a new psychologist and emerging leader (note what's missing—judgmental absolutes such as "this will ALWAYS be the case," "I'll NEVER have time or freedom to date").
- In my early thirties, I was feeling overwhelmed but also devoted to investing in my sister and her new son as she navigated young, single motherhood and we both determined how to live life as newly minted "half orphans" (note what's missing—judgment toward the circumstances in my life I didn't choose; instead, when the judgments crept up, I took the time to investigate the real emotions behind them).
- At various times throughout this period of my life I felt helpless, sorrowful, angry, despaired, dazed, joyful, content, peaceful, bitter, hurt, lost, satisfied, dissatisfied . . . I could probably fill this chapter with the abundance of emotions I've felt in this place of singleness (note what's missing—judgments about why I felt those emotions or that I shouldn't be feeling them, as well as all-or-nothing thinking that told me I couldn't successfully live my life unless those emotions were absent).
- Finally, another accurate descriptor I reminded myself of was that a dating/marriage relationship would not permanently eliminate all these experiences and emotions (note what's missing—*assumptions*).

So you see, radical acceptance is complicated but also deeply affirming and freeing.

I want to circle back to our experience of emotions for a second. This is a place where I find most people get tripped up or desperately want to avoid, minimize, or judge, because let's be honest, unpleasant emotions are TOUGH. However, it's important to note that no emotion is ever wrong. When I share this with people I often get pushback. "But what if the emotion is based on my inadequate or incorrect interpretation of a situation?" Or the more frequent "But what if I don't want to or *shouldn't* be feeling this emotion?" Radical acceptance

> If you're feeling an emotion, you're feeling an emotion, end of story.

necessitates that we get past the conclusion that certain emotions should never be felt, are incorrect, or must be avoided at all costs (that last one single-handedly keeps me in business). If you're feeling an emotion, you're feeling an emotion, end of story. Now, what you *do* with that emotion is an entirely different conversation and something we'll cover in the next chapter. Here's what I typically see happens with emotions when individuals are under the impression that these emotions they are encountering are wrong:

1. The emotion stems from judgment. "I want to feel confident and loved in my singleness but I'm feeling lonely and insecure. What is WRONG with me!" or the ever-popular "I'll NEVER be able to feel differently!"
2. The emotion becomes an identity. Instead of feeling insecure, we make a tiny tweak to that action verb of "feeling" and switch it out with a linking verb. Remember third-grade grammar? Linking verbs demonstrate a relationship between a subject and a descriptor of that subject. So, "I feel insecure" becomes "I AM insecure."

Voila! You've just created a new identity for yourself. I'll see you in my office next week (also, we're going to address this head-on in chapter 9).

All right, let's review the ingredients to effective radical acceptance, because this skill is absolutely foundational to the practice of embracing uncomfortable.

- Describe, in detail, your present circumstances.
- Avoid (or go back and remove) judgments including condemning language, all-or-nothing statements (never/always), and "shoulds" or "if-onlys."
- Be honest—do not minimize or deny what is happening.
- Eliminate assumptions or opinions you cannot back up with fact.

Now, let's put what you've read so far into action. Take a moment to define a current experience or situation you're in and attempt to do so with the rules of radical acceptance.

Well done! You get a gold star! You've accomplished the most essential element of embracing uncomfortable and a task we will frequently return to as we journey through the various steps required to live out your authentic purpose. And, no doubt, you'll begin to see its necessity and consequently its challenge in many areas of your life now. Don't fret . . . we're doing this together. Rome wasn't built in a day and neither were you. Before you move on to the next chapter, take a few days, maybe a week or even a month* and try practicing radical acceptance. If you journal, try writing out this practice and reframing anything that falls outside

---

* But please come back, trust me—transformation looks good on you!

the boundaries. If you are more the verbal processing type, share with a safe and trusted friend/loved one what you are attempting to do and be open to their feedback. Once you've begun to grasp the elements of radical acceptance, then you're ready to move on to the next chapter.

7

BALANCING FEELINGS AND FACTS

val·i·da·tion | \ ˈva-lə-ˈdā-shən:
recognizing the impact of both the feelings we encounter in a given moment as well as the presence of objective evidence—both carry significance and both matter.

What emotion(s) do you try your darndest to avoid, and how is that impacting your ability, or lack thereof, to move toward transformation?

I used to lead a therapy group for clients struggling with what we call "emotional regulation." The individuals in my group fell on the spectrum of navigating heightened levels of anxiety, isolating depression, or expressive anger. Each week we would spend time processing how their reactions to emotions impacted their ability to communicate effectively, maintain healthy relationships, and engage in successful decision-making. Group members came to the session each week with a vivid variety of illustrations showing how their emotions had triggered unhealthy responses to various situations. While each story represented the unique encounter, personality, and situation of the teller, I began to notice a common theme among their shared experiences: emotions produced one of two responses—expression or isolation. Members of the group either expressed these feelings with intense, often impulsive reactions, or they isolated them, choosing to ignore the feeling or dismiss its significance. It was all either/or extremes. A balanced common ground that allowed them the space to feel and validate their emotions while still expressing them through healthy, regulated responses was foreign territory.

> Without the experience of deep pain, we can never truly know what overwhelming joy feels like.

THE TRAP OF EMOTIONAL THINKING

While this particular group of individuals was extreme in their treatment of emotions, this phenomenon is something I see (and personally experience) quite often. I jokingly tell my new clients that whether they know it or not, they usually have an unconscious expectation at the start of counseling that I'll be able to remove any future experience of negative, unpleasant, *uncomfortable* emotions permanently from their lives from here to eternity. If only I was that good a therapist.

First of all, that would make me a TERRIBLE therapist. Without the experience of deep pain, we can never truly know what overwhelming joy feels like. It's sort of like growing up in Phoenix and now living in Chicago; I'd never know what blistering heat and bone-chilling cold could possibly feel like without the trial of surviving in both environments during summer and winter. Not only do our emotions give us insight on how to interpret our relationships, circumstances, and situations, but they also assist us in comprehending what other emotions mean. I wouldn't know what peace is without experiencing anger. I wouldn't understand excitement without encountering dread. Love is more fully experienced when we can also comprehend loss. Yet we're constantly fighting to avoid the uncomfortable out of fear that it will overtake us and, as you've read by now, that leaves us living in a place of inauthenticity, reaction, and disengagement.

I see this play out a lot with my clients in all manner of life circumstances. One client in particular was struggling in her marriage, feeling alone, misunderstood, and invalidated.* Partly because of that, she'd tripped into the unexpected position of an extramarital affair. Now she was trapped in a fear cycle. She wanted to save her marriage but felt terrified that it couldn't develop into what she hoped and dreamed of. She also feared losing the momentary bliss and excitement of the extramarital relationship, knowing it couldn't be sustained for the long haul. Both sides of the coin were being dictated and controlled by emotion. On the one side, her behavior, fueled by fear, continued to play out as increasing conflict with her spouse because of uncommunicated and, therefore, unmet expectations. On the other side was the cycle of pursuing, then breaking, the connection of her relationship outside the marriage out of fear that it wouldn't last, but then fearing that it was the only alternative to her unfulfilling marriage, and so it went . . .

For my single clients longing for relationship, the circle of emotional decision-making looks a lot like this: "I desire a relationship

---

* To all my single people out there struggling with the same experiences and emotions, I pray you know the depth of these feelings don't go away with a marriage certificate.

and feel lonely, rejected, unlovable, and depressed as a result of being in my current circumstances." The unfortunate consequence can be seeking solace among partners who fail (significantly) to meet their standards, isolating themselves in the comfort of home (which then fails to move them in the direction they desire), or just perceiving life as an overall disappointment of possibilities because this one unattainable goal continues to elude them. Again, either way you flip the coin, insulated emotional thinking is the ultimate culprit.

The other pattern I often encounter is working with individuals who've been deeply hurt by past relationships, whether it be parents or other members in their family of origin, spouses, friends, past romantic partners, or even coworkers. The words or actions that occurred in the dynamic of these connections have left scars in the form of false identities, unhealthy motivations, and/or inaccurate expectations of their influence on or reaction from others. Their emotions scream "Run, hide, retreat, or avoid." So they do, plowing over anyone and everything on their way toward a safe and secure—but false—moment of bliss.

Regardless of the circumstances, the shared outcome in the above illustrations is people living out of emotional thinking—rather than intentional direction based on alignment with our values and purpose.

Let's break this down a bit more concretely. Our concepts of value and purpose come from the cognitive process of thinking and reflection. Thoughts can be simply defined as ideas, opinions, and beliefs we have about the world around us—but also about ourselves and what we define as central to our motivations and how we engage the everyday circumstances of our lives.

Not sure what those are in your life? This is the perfect time to take a purposeful pause and jot down what comes to mind. If it's hard to come up with ideas, ask a friend. Or your mom. She'd love to hear from you anyway.

These ideas, opinions, and beliefs aren't always that obvious. Take note of what you're believing of yourself and others when stuff hits the fan and you find yourself in one of those circumstances once again. If we *don't* declare our values and purpose, it's too easy to allow other people, circumstances, or situations to declare them for us. And those declarations are rooted in overlooked emotions. Too many times I've worked with clients who act on "values" or a "purpose" that others have placed upon them. While they want to value excellence, persistence, honesty, or balance, instead they seem to relapse into negative values of failure, powerlessness, weakness, or inadequacy.

> Too often I've worked with clients who act on "values" or a "purpose" that others have placed on them.

DON'T DROWN IN THE SEA OF EMOTIONS

When I speak to groups of people, I often use this analogy to illustrate the impact of how we get stuck when we function exclusively in the realm of emotional decision-making, and also why radical acceptance, as we discussed in chapter 6, is so critical to our ability to embrace uncomfortable. One of the larger tourism initiatives in the city of Chicago over the last several years has been the beautification of the Chicago River and the creation of the Riverwalk along the waterway through downtown. Living in the city, I love walking the Riverwalk as part of my route to work or enjoying a warm summer evening stroll with the view of the city reflecting off the water. In fact, our previous mayor, Rahm

Emanuel, once said that Lake Michigan is the Yellowstone of Chicago and the Chicago River is our Grand Canyon.[1] However, as beautiful as the river is from the views looking down on it, the fact remains that it's still fairly polluted. In July 2017, summer storms deposited 2.6 billion gallons of bacteria-laden sewage and runoff into the river.

So let's say I'm enjoying one of those summer-night strolls and along the way an inconsiderate and oblivious jogger happens to run into me and knock me off my balance, sending me tripping over the edge and splash-dab in the middle of 2.6 billion gallons of bacteria-laden sewage. Not an ideal situation. I can imagine my immediate reaction would be one of shock, fear, and anger. Also, this is completely **unfair**! I didn't choose to get slammed into by the jogger or topple into the river. This has completely ruined my Friday night plans, to say the least, and with the focus on those thoughts my anger at the injustice of it all intensifies.

Here's the catch: if all I do is focus on the feelings (I feel anxious, I feel enraged, I feel disbelief), the reality of my surroundings and the actions necessary to get me out of them fail to fall on my radar, and I quickly drown in a sea (or river) of emotions. I don't want to be wading in the depths of this river right now—despite how legendary you are, Chicago, I don't want to be stuck in your river! But I'm here! It's my current reality. And denying or minimizing that reality or hyper-focusing on what got me there in the first place is not going to do anything to get me out. No, my only hope of resolving this situation is to first radically accept where I'm at (the river), determine where I want to go (OUT), acknowledge my emotions (fear, anxiety, anger) as part of the driving force behind my actions, but also consider the facts that it's going to take a swim or a scream for help to get me to shore. The ability to embrace uncomfortable to live according to our values and purpose means truthfully interpreting our *circumstances* **and** our *emotions*. I'm in the river—I may not want to be here, I may not have chosen the circumstances that put me here, I may not like the options for getting me to where I want to go—but here I am, so what do I want to do next?

How do we apply the river analogy to our daily lives? Let me give you another example. One of my friends is in a position at her work where she leads a team of people who depend on her to complete their responsibilities effectively. Over the past several months she's been tasked with a significant project her firm is depending on for success, and she's struggling to keep her head above water with her existing responsibilities. Meanwhile, the team who reports to her is also angling for her time, focus, attention, and direction. These two competing priorities, the demands of this new project and the responsibility to lead and support her team, represent the river she's currently ~~drowning~~ floating in. In our recent conversations, it's been evident that my friend's behavior is motivated by the "feeling anchors" of fear (of failure) and intense anxiety (I'm not enough). The emotional experience is powerful and perhaps even overwhelming, leading to physical consequences, since anxiety can lead to a physical manifestation of symptoms such as increased heart rate, nausea, digestive problems, and chest pain. Add to that restlessness, tension, racing thoughts, and fear, and my friend has been logging longer hours, losing sleep, cutting off social connections, and not taking care of her body with regular exercise and healthier eating. The emotions of fear and anxiety are driving her decision-making and pushing her *against* the current and away from shore, not *toward* the dry land of her values and purpose.

As we talked recently, I challenged her to pause and consider what her foundational values are and what she sees as her core purpose. While she struggled to articulate them exactly in that moment, she could see that her current choices were far from what she valued most. Changing her behavior was going to require the daily discipline of choosing her actions and reactions based on filtering them through the grid of her values and purpose, instead of exclusively through the sieve of her emotions.

THE DISCIPLINE OF BALANCED PERSPECTIVE

Following this practice was going to take a real commitment to embracing uncomfortable. She recognized the need to go to her boss and request either help with, or release from, some of the more demanding responsibilities of this new project. The thought of having this conversation was in itself terrifying and anxiety-provoking. Her initial reaction was "I can't do that!" So we paused here and circled back to her other options. Could she stop responding to her direct reports? No, that wasn't an option either. Was the pace at which she was working endurable? No, she stated clearly, she was at her breaking point. As we weighed each decision for its loss and its gain, she began to see where the choice to align with her values was going to mean taking a momentary hit that was likely to feel extremely uncomfortable. However, as she oriented herself to the losses she *wasn't* willing to endure (her health, her relationships, her *sanity*), she became more open to the reality that stepping toward and embracing the uncomfortable decision of setting a boundary at work, regardless of the consequence, was ultimately the most important thing.

This practice is the *discipline of balanced perspective*. While our brain is equally wired to consider the emotional impact and the factual information influencing each of our decisions, we tend to lean more in one direction or the other. We're going to focus on those who fall more frequently in the emotional-decision-making department. The consequence of orienting ourselves to just the emotion means we're choosing to pursue options that often fail to align with what is really most important to us. The choice to embrace uncomfortable necessitates that we pursue a balanced consideration of both.

When we allow just our emotions to direct our decisions, all of a sudden things that might be considered speed bumps, where we can slow down and choose to proceed with caution, become concrete walls. "Guess I'll be late to work—again." "I'm too anxious" and "I can't" or "I have no other choice" become inseparable, and we speed toward decisions that leave our values and purpose spinning in the dust.

Let's use a story from another chapter to play this out more concretely. Remember coffee-shop lady? I'm going to put myself in her angry shoes for a moment. So I'm stuck in this line watching someone personalize their order like a six-year-old at the Build-A-Bear Workshop, and the clock is ticking down the minutes of my wiggle room to arrive on time to my next appointment. My emotions of impatience and anxiety are getting the best of me, and I'm tempted to make some snide remark or gesture in order to get the point across that I'm running late and this tea-ordering approach is quite inconsiderate to the customers behind her. If I *only* consider my emotions, that is *likely* how I'm going to react!

> Facts influence rational decision-making and are the counterpoint to our emotional motivators.

THE COUNTERPOINT TO
OUR EMOTIONAL MOTIVATORS

However, my values and purpose don't fall in the circle of emotional thinking. Sure, they might have initially been motivated by emotional experiences and they might evoke emotion when I'm functioning fully in them. Nevertheless, if they truly represent what is most important to me in any given moment, then they fall in the category of *fact*. Facts influence rational decision-making and are the counterpoint to our emotional motivators. "I value relationships" is a factual statement that represents a priority in my life. It's not an opinion, something wavering that can be influenced by the situation and circumstance. If I play out the balanced input of both my emotions, frustration and impatience, and my factual values, relationship, allowing both to affect my response, I'm more likely to recognize and react in a way that truly represents the core of who I am. Allowing these feelings to shed insight to my present circumstance is important. Those emotions help me understand my internal reactions—"I'm running late." "It's important to me to be on time" (or more likely, "I place a lot of value in what others think of me, and I don't want to be seen as a flake or not valuing others' time"). However, my rational thought, based on fact, also needs its five minutes of fame: "I value relationship." A disgruntled reaction here moves me away from those things that represent what is most significant to me."

Now, the next step is to find a balanced response that considers both influences, emotion and fact. So instead of huffing and puffing, I take a deep, cleansing breath, smile at the woman in front of me, wait with at least attempted patience, and when it is my turn at the counter, I deliberately slow my words (the opposite of an aggravated response) and show authentic kindness to the harried barista behind the counter.

Okay, let's be honest. This is not going to work every time. Don't set yourself up for failure here. I'm REAL good at knowing my values . . . I'm so-so at implementing them in the moment. As most of us are. That's why I like to say "practice makes better."

THE VENN DIAGRAM

Balancing facts and feelings is like the overlapping circles of a Venn diagram.[2] One circle says "fact: this is where I'm at." We call it rationality. It's logical, tangible, real. It's without judgment, not good or bad. And the other circle says "feeling: I have emotions related to this experience in this circle over here. I feel angry, I feel bitter, I feel hurt, I feel ashamed, I feel unworthy." And, like your rational thoughts and experiences, your emotional thoughts and experiences *just are*. Not good or bad/right or wrong. So, if my married client were to consider her circumstances through this lens, she might say, "I'm afraid, I'm angry, I'm lonely, and I feel hopeless." She has to determine her values, and, importantly, only she gets to have the final say on defining those. Let's say she settles on the desire to stay in her marriage, then that becomes her fact. "I value the sanctity of marriage in this situation, and I want to pursue healing in my relationship by first letting go of my affair, then coming clean to my husband, and requesting counseling to repair the damage we've both encountered and caused." The feelings are completely valid, but they don't exclusively determine the outcome. Her next steps align with the influence of both, and she's going to continue dancing between them as she moves toward the pursuit of marital healing.

The same is true for my single friends. I hear them communicate the following: "Emotionally, I feel lonely at times, insecure at times, confident at times, fearful, overwhelmed, jealous of my married friends." On the factual side, they express that they're single and busy and older, and the pool of quality individuals is smaller than it was in college. It may take encouragement, but as they consider what they really value, their honesty often communicates that a healthy relationship based on shared values, honest communication, and mutual respect is a greater priority than a Friday-night hookup. Once again, the dance between the emotions and the facts is a consistent one. It is important to hold fast to the truth that neither circle is lost or forsaken in this practice.

> The feeling that you've truly been seen and heard is a remarkable motivator.

I want to add a quick word on the importance of validation. A whole book could be written on the importance of feeling validated—feeling seen, feeling heard, feeling understood in our thoughts and emotions. We're going to discuss the most significant barriers to change in the next chapter, but when it comes to validation, we confuse validation for agreement. Here's an example. If I say, "You've put a lot of hard work into this" when I'm not keen on the outcome, I have a fear the other person is hearing "you did a great job!" So instead I focus on the deficiencies, the failures, the places where *my* expectations haven't been met.

Do you know what the most common theme is among my clients when asked the question, "What's been most transformative for you in our work together?" Almost without fail they respond with "You've heard my concerns and validated my experiences." Sure, the problem-solver in me cringes a bit when the #1 answer isn't "You've helped me conquer what I thought was an insurmountable goal!" Yet, with pause, I realize that *is* overcoming an obstacle. The feeling that you've truly been seen and heard, the foundation of validation, is a remarkable motivator. Think about it. In your moments of greatest security, what is one of the key conditions you encountered? Chances are it's a sense of validation—of worthiness. That's what validation does. It gives you and the people around you a sense of worth. Together, let's be stewards of the privilege of reflecting back to ourselves and to those in our inner circles the merit of their presence. Give it a shot—increase your validation vocabulary.

8

JUSTIFICATION, MINIMIZATION, AND DENIAL

ob·struc·tion | \ əb-ˈstrək-shən:
the barriers we unconsciously (or consciously) implement
that prevent us from embracing uncomfortable and
experiencing real transformation in our lives.

*What persistent patterns of behavior
prevent you from engaging in new ways of
thinking, acting, and/or relating to others?*

I live in this amazing loft apartment on the edge of downtown Chicago. It was a killer Craigslist find, and I love every quirky element of the space. However, one thing I've learned living in the city is you'll never exactly find every item on your list of "must-haves" when it comes to residential space. For the gain of open-concept living, a modern kitchen (oh hey there, you wonderful dishwasher you), and the most cozy, beautiful built-in book nook, I had to dance-battle it out with my roommate (and best friend) for the doorless (but windowed) walk-in closet pretending to be a bedroom, or the master, but windowless, space. I got the room that fits my bed . . . and nothing else. Ah, city living. At least I have a window to see you through.

In order to get creative with clothing storage, I had to purchase several pieces of furniture to substitute for the closet I was *sleeping in* instead of containing my belongings therein. Forever in search of a good deal and a chance to transform something old into something newer, I found an unbelievable armoire at the local Salvation Army. Somehow, I managed to convince said roommate (and best friend) that "we're modern women, we can do hard things" and traipsed her down to the thrift shop with her midsize SUV. Once inside, she took a good look at the 8x4 foot piece of *solid wood furniture*, side-eyed me, and said with the ultimate exasperation, "There is absolutely NO WAY just the two of us are capable of managing Narnia's wardrobe on our own, let alone fitting it into my car. Square peg plus round hole equals . . . you do the shapes."

My response: "It's not *that* big." I should mention I have the spiritual gift of cunning and justification, so a few more side-eyes and $70 later, the Salvation Army guys had rolled the armoire out the doors and left it on the sidewalk ("that's as far as we go, ma'am").

Problem number one occurred when said roommate and best friend was right about the armoire not fitting in her car. That thing didn't have a prayer of squeezing into the trunk of a car that, if I was lucky, could hold a small coffee table, a Costco crate of cherries, and a yoga mat. My solution: get a bigger car! This would require leaving her alone* on the sidewalk in front of the store in the middle of August, in ninety-degree heat, to guard the armoire

---

* *"Abandoned" is the term she prefers.*

and fend off all the thrift-store vultures who were also in search of the best armoire deal that day. I blessed her with a bag of Cheetos, promised her my firstborn, and drove to the nearest U-Haul, where I rented a truck and a dolly.

The amount of maneuvering and the extra good-Samaritan shopper hands that sucker required to get into the back of the rented pickup truck should have somehow convinced me of the unlikelihood we could get it out of the truck, *and* up the steep flight of stairs leading into our second-floor apartment. It didn't. Also, I failed to mention a crucial detail to the sacrifice of city living—no elevator. We're modern women! Elevator, schmelavator. I was confident that we could do it. The roommate (and best friend) did protest. That armoire must have weighed two hundred pounds, "But we're modern women and we can do hard things!" One hour, more curse words than I care to admit, a fair amount of yelling, one desperate cry of "I'm going to pass out!" and frantic pleas to "not let go or I'll DIE!" later, we got that beautiful, big baby through the door.

I think my roommate (and my best friend)* gave me the side-eye for the rest of the week. Also, I was banned from thrift stores, buying large pieces of furniture, and using the term modern women in any connection to lifting or moving anything between this day and high-fiving Peter at the pearly gates. She made me sign a notarized paper napkin *with those exact words on it.*

OUR THREE BIGGEST OBSTACLES

The armoire adventure of 2014 is a great example of a trap I can easily find myself in, an unwillingness to change my perspective through the stubborn practices of justification, minimization,

---

* Okay, she's still my best friend but it was really touch and go for a while there.

and/or denial, the three biggest obstacles that derail us from choosing consistent with our values and acting according to our purpose (also known as the three haters to change). Side-eyed roommate/best friend offered numerous tidbits of wisdom throughout the journey to bring armoire to its new home. "It's too big, it's too heavy, we're modern but our muscles aren't up-to-date." To which I responded, "It's not *that* big" (minimization), "It's not heavy" (denial), "You said my arms are looking more toned since I started working out last week, so we can definitely do this" (justification). Before we jump into explore these concepts further, let's take a quick step back and review the ingredients required for transformation.

As I mentioned in chapter 7, in my work I frequently shift between a posture of validation and being a cheerleader of change as my clients open themselves to the vulnerability of their circumstances and their desires for growth. Our ability to transform into those growth areas requires a willingness to step into both. Coaching clients to implement a practice of self-validation is often healing and brings the release of shame and self-loathing. Often, they've spent years beating themselves up for the feelings they've experienced, filling their minds with those dreadful "shouldn'ts," trapped in the past of *their* choices or the consequence of others'. Change is and will always be the trickier path. Validation is a surrender to permission, allowing yourself the green light to experience the emotions of your actions and the grief, anger, pain, or disappointment of how others have failed you.

Change is always harder. Back in chapter 5 we discussed how our brain is like water—without intentionality it will default to the path of least resistance. One of the reasons we are so quick to give up on change is the process it takes to alter habitual patterns of action (think back to our analogy of the wheat fields: forging new pathways takes determined persistence). Another reason is we're simply ignorant to the factors keeping us in our present holding pattern. We're conditioned to the art of unconscious decision-making, and we need to bring awareness to the forefront of our minds. In short, we need to know when and why to embrace the uncomfortable. We've taken that first step by intentionally defining our core values and our overarching purpose. Now we need

> Denial is falling into the river and refusing to accept that you're there.

to clarify what obstacles we can expect to present themselves in the process of our transformation.

Justification keeps us stuck in our circumstances because we convince ourselves that the outcomes *will be different this time* despite any stimulating change. Minimization is deceiving ourselves of the impact of our current circumstances. It's saying, "It's not that big of a deal (the stairs aren't *that* steep)." Denial is most often focused on our contributions to the present moment and is also the opposite of radical acceptance. Denial is falling into the river and refusing to accept that you're there.

Before we dive into exploring these concepts, you need to know one thing. This process is going to require humility, whether you've chosen where you are at today or you haven't.* That might necessitate a practice of grieving and lamentation before you're ready to swim in the current of change. What exactly do I mean by that? Let me give you an example. I've worked with a lot of clients who've been hurt by the ruthless damage of trauma. The destructive actions of others have shattered their sense of self,

---

* When in doubt, say this cheer: "my location isn't my destination." Believe it and onward you go.

their approach to the world around them, and their perspective of what is truth. This is a place where justification is warranted. They are *justified* in their feelings but often find themselves trapped in their circumstances. There is no greater need for validation than in the depths of trauma grief. Minimizing the pain to push forward in the present often means they are just stepping deeper into the water without the knowledge of how to swim.

Grief and lament are powerful experiences that say, "This was not how it was supposed to be and because of that I feel _____." Note the period at the end of that sentence. You feel _____. There is no should or should not, like or don't like, want to or don't want to. Your feeling(s) simply is or are. Please know I don't see it as fair or reasonable that you may have to engage this process through the scars of trauma. As I do with my clients, I grieve alongside you and together we build the momentum of a stronger current to step into this place of transformation together. So, if you need to pause here, no matter how long, please do so. But do so with the commitment to humbly step back into the process—your process.

Now let's talk about humility for a minute. In the world of nouns, humility gets a bad rap in my opinion. Too often we fail to see humility as a choice and instead see it as a weakness, or worse, a state of resignation. The best definitions of humility include one essential word: freedom. Humility is being free to view things from different angles, to consider other options without the false belief that it will rob us of our identity. Let me set you up with the honest expectation that humility might trigger your anxiety. It's an Indiana Jones–level leap of faith and at its core, the practice of humility is very much the choice to embrace uncomfortable. What keeps most people from this place is actually the first barrier to change . . . justification.

JUSTIFICATION:
LETTING YOURSELF OFF THE HOOK

There is no better way to ensure you stay in the holding pattern of habit than justification. Years ago, I was working with a client who was battling chronic low-grade depression and a resulting lack of motivation. She envisioned her life looking significantly different than the outcome she was experiencing in the present, but struggled to embrace the uncomfortable choices necessary to ignite a path of change in her life. Approaching fifty, she was hoping to be married with children, or at least thriving in her consulting career with a strong community of deep relationships that brought her fulfillment and joy and steady plans on a Friday night. Instead, she was in the depths of another breakup (the third in two years), failing to find joy or interest in her present place of employment (and honestly her career choices overall), and frequently found herself at home binging on empty calories and emptier reality TV shows, or worse, at the local dive bar trolling for guys.

Every week she would present with the same desire for a different outcome—a meaningful relationship being number one. Now, let me pause here and clarify, as a single woman who in high school anticipated celebrating double-digit anniversaries and having children by now, I could relate and empathize greatly with her current grief and sense of loss over something highly valued and desired that had yet to materialize in her life. Honestly acknowledging and sitting with the pain of unmet expectations and heart-longings was a critical element of our work together. However, it's also a place we can easily get stuck in. For some reason, we mistake steps toward change as a betrayal of our emotions and our circumstances. If I change my pattern of behavior, I'm basically admitting I was wrong or inadequate to begin with (which is SO not true—but we'll get there). It's kind of like mistaking validation for agreement. The outcome? We dig in our heels and continue defending whatever choices we've made that led to our present circumstances. We justify, often out of self-protection and fear that if we choose to do differently, then the only person we have to blame for our present circumstances is ourselves. For my client, that meant an ongoing pattern of unhealthy relationships because she justified that any type of companionship was better than the option of being alone. Yet, when faced with the truth of her actions as we processed each week, she consistently expressed frustration and anger toward the quality and behavior of the men in her life. Justification was a prison, trapping her in an endless cycle of bitterness and disappointment. When the options her heart longed for didn't present themselves, instead of shifting her perspective to see different opportunities that might bring alternate forms of fulfillment, she returned to the familiar habit of unhealthy decisions with justification, maintaining her position on the hamster wheel of life.

Here's the deal. We ALL justify. Just think about your last argument with your spouse, or the last conversation you had with a coworker who graciously expressed concern or questions about your directional choices on a project or vision, or the last time you decided to skip the gym, or when you had *just another* drink, or said "no" to your kid because you just "didn't want to." My hunch is the follow-up internal conversation swirling around in your head was chock-full of justification. Why do we do this? Because justification is an attempt to let ourselves off the hook and avoid the uncomfortable rest shifting around within us. If you think back to the last time you justified, it is likely because you weren't following your values and were misaligned with your purpose (even if you haven't fully defined those yet). We have no need to justify the choices we feel confident in or pleased with—the emotional payback is justification enough (joy, assurance, peace). However, when the resulting emotions are less pleasurable, we'll often resort to all kinds of stratagems to convince ourselves that our actions were defensible.

How, then, do we step out of the hamster wheel? The first step is to hit the brakes and take a pause (if you're asking yourself how to do this, clearly you wheeled right past chapter 5). Justification can come so quickly we fail to see or recognize its behavior until the situation has come and gone and we're left dealing with the shame or regret of another impulsive response. Pausing creates space for reflection when we encounter the prickly feel of an uncomfortable reaction. The goal is to get to the place where that reaction is recognized internally before it shifts to an external expression.

This comes with time, patience, and practice. Again, commit to a pattern of pausing now before any hints of justification present themselves. Then, once they do, you've already got a new habit in place. In your space of reflection, look for makers of justification. "I was tired." "She was wrong." "He was harsh." "That wasn't fair." "I'm always the one taken advantage of." The key is to see where you are excusing your behavior, thoughts, or reactions. Avoid labeling them as right or wrong. In the process of reducing the justification in your life, you also want to decrease the time you spend in your internal *People's Court*. Once you've hooked justification, consider where you need to label an emotional experience and validate it. Shifting from justification to validation is a powerful way to acknowledge yourself and your experience without contributing to the baggage of unproductive rationalizations, or, worse, resignation. Shifting looks like this:

Justification: "She **always** reacts that way, so it doesn't really matter. I'm going to do it however I want to."

Validation: "I feel **disappointed** when she sees my actions as intentionally disrespectful."

Justification: "I **never** have enough time to do the things I want to do."

Validation: "I feel **frustrated** that the other responsibilities in my life seem to take priority over the things I enjoy."

Justification: "It's never going to change so why bother trying."

Validation: "I feel **tired**, **angry**, and **discouraged** that the system continues to treat me and others this way."

Moving from justification to validation means you aren't dismissing your experience or the feelings that result from it. They are valid, even if they're based on a misunderstanding or a misinterpretation of others. Feelings are feelings—stop judging them. Once you've let yourself feel, then it's time to reorient yourself to where you want to be. This can trigger those dreadful justifications all over again. So, if you find yourself stuck in the negative loop cycle, keep reminding yourself of the feeling and continue pressing toward the willingness to embrace the uncomfortable. You'll navigate out of justification eventually!

"IT'S NOT THAT BIG OF A DEAL"

Now let's talk minimization. Minimization is just a fancy way of saying "it's not that big of a deal." It's sort of the cousin of justification. If justification says, "I'm doing it this way because of someone or something else;" minimization says, "My choices or responses aren't impacting me or others that much." Or, the ever popular "it's not that much of a problem." If you'll bear with me for a hot second, I'll explain things in the form of a grammar lesson (yes, this book provides psychological advice, medical wisdom, and now language arts training—you're welcome. Also, thank you, middle-school grammar teacher. You were right; we *would* need this in the future). Justification is all about conjunction words—that is, the words that link two parts of a sentence together. The common culprit of justification is the conjunction *because*. Minimization is all about the adverbs: *really, most, however, usually*. While minimization can look a lot like justification, the big difference is that justification is putting the root of the problem on someone else while minimization at least acknowledges your role in the consequences you're experiencing, but you've convinced yourself that they're not really causing any palpable damage.

Often it's years of minimization that land clients in my office, uncertain of what the real root of their pain is but knowing something's not functioning properly in their lives. The language of minimization is "It *really* doesn't happen that often." "Usually, I respond differently." "*Most* of the time I'm able to control it." "I can see the problem; however, it's not affecting me that much."

I used to call myself the queen of justification, but over the years I've realized minimization is really my drug of choice, *especially* when it comes to the things I say yes to. I used to work with an executive coach who had to gently yet firmly remind me quite often that my personality and leadership style rarely lends itself to rest and intentionally pausing (you can imagine how uncomfortable writing about and practicing the discipline of pausing was for me). I say yes because I see the potential in new opportunities and get overly excited. Then, when my calendar is full and I have little breathing room, I simply tell myself I'm not *really* THAT overcommitted and while I have a lot of responsibilities, most of the time I'm managing just fine and it's not really impacting me or others too much.

Sound familiar to anyone? Minimization is sneaky because we *are* acknowledging the problem—we're just downplaying its impact. It's like a quarterback telling his coach the strain in his shoulder doesn't hurt that much and isn't a big deal, only to go for a sixty-yard throw and, in the process, tear his rotator cuff, putting him out for the season, or worse, ending his career. Since we're willingly acknowledging the problem, minimization can be challenging to change. We *know* what's wrong, we just don't want to admit or accept it because change might equate to saying no to or removing ourselves from something that does bring a level of gratification and comfort (momentarily).

> Minimization is sneaky because we *are* acknowledging the problem—we're just downplaying its impact.

Overcoming the obstacle of minimization in order to embrace the uncomfortable *requires* that we know our values. So, if you struggled in chapter 4, time to go back and read it again. Here's a great example of why. Every year in my Professional Identity and Ethical Practice course, I take my students through a values exercise designed to help them see what they are prioritizing in their lives and what decisions they're making that might be grossly misaligned with what is really most important to them. The first step in this exercise is to write down any item that comes to mind that they believe they need to function effectively every day. Without fail, the most popular answer is a smartphone. However, as the exercise progresses, students are asked to reflect on and identify other areas of importance to them through various prompts that challenge them to consider influential people in their lives, critical memories, places of significance, and deeply desired goals. Then, because I value authenticity in every area of my life, I challenge them to get uncomfortable. They have to start eliminating what they've written until the number of things that take prominence in their lives is whittled down to five (much like what I challenged you to do in exploring your own values). Guess what almost always goes first? The smartphone. Yet the average person spends over four hours a day on that little device![1] We minimize the impact or time spent on it, despite its inconsistency with our values. However, without knowing what our values really are, we have no way to gauge where are choices might be falsely aligned.

Once you do have a clear grasp on your values and purpose, it's much "easier" (put in quotations because, come on, we're talking about getting uncomfortable here—it's NEVER easy) to identify the shifts in our behavior that need to take place. At this point it becomes a matter of defining and avoiding the significant losses that can result from our decisions. Remember our conversation around the principle that all decisions involve loss? If Mr. Quarterback values excellence and sees his purpose as engaging in every effort to the fullest capacity of his giftings and talents, acknowledging the intensity of his pain and losing the opportunity to play in a high-stakes game is a *lesser* loss than the totality of a season or his entire career. In short, he would be choosing to be a better steward of his gifting and talents. Conversely, his decision to minimize and step into the game would represent a divergence from his core values and purpose. Instead of pausing for purpose, he paused for praise. He made a decision that would bring him satisfaction in the moment.

"IT REALLY WON'T TAKE *THAT* MUCH TIME . . ."

Let me use myself as an example. A few days before writing this chapter, I received a phone call from someone asking about my interest in an influential leadership role at a local organization I am involved with. The guy on the phone might as well have been speaking my love language. The expectations and possible experiences involved everything I love and seemed to speak directly to some of my key strengths. Saying yes would likely mean some amazing opportunities to join forces with other change agents in ways that carried the potential to enact sustainable transformation in my beloved city of Chicago. As we continued to speak about the responsibilities a yes entailed, I found myself in that familiar place of minimization. "It really won't *take* that much time away from what I've already committed to," runs the rationale. Thankfully, a disciplined practice I've committed to held me accountable to choosing consistent with my values instead of caving to minimization. I responded with "This sounds like an awesome opportunity, thank you for even considering me as an option for this role. I'd like to take forty-eight hours to consider things before I get back to you with a definitive answer."

Old Deb would respond to the emotional moment (Excitement! Intrigue! Mild guilt at the thought of saying no and letting someone down!). Deb who's writing a book and wants to (and sees the value in) practice what she preaches chose the discipline of practicing the pause. In those forty-eight hours, intentional reflection on what responsibilities I already hold, the number of people I'm already accountable to, and the time left for rest, fellowship, and errand-running helped me see the truth that I wasn't being honest about the reality of my free time. Another yes, no matter how good (read: comfortable) it might feel in the moment, would conflict with both my values and my purpose. So I made the briefly uncomfortable choice of saying no.

Here's the thing: I KNOW I let some people down with that decision and I may have even left them in a difficult bind.

However, that doesn't mean my decision was wrong and if my character is consistent, once the emotional impact of my "no" subsides, they'll know that, if they don't already. We have to allow others to feel the consequences of our decision even if we don't like the feelings they encounter.* We also have to stick to those decisions, if we've really considered and been honest with ourselves about how they align with or skew from our values and purpose, despite the effects they might have on others.

Before we move on to denial, I want to look at minimization from another angle—minimizing emotional pain resulting from trauma. Trauma is very real and very present in our current world. Unfortunately, I've seen many people minimizing the impact of trauma on their lives because they believe it's either too much to process or because they don't think they'll be able to function if they really step into the depths of their hurt. If you've encountered trauma in your life, minimizing the experience(s) and the impression it has left on you is like bandaging a wound that ultimately needs surgery to heal. Can you function with a bandage? Maybe, at least for a little while. Does surgery hurt and require more intensive and enduring healing time? Yes. Does surgery leave a scar? Yes. If you're minimizing the impact of a gaping wound, I first want to acknowledge your bravery and commitment, and the roots of injustice at the heart of the losses you're faced to choose between. Then I want to encourage you to pursue healing.

DENIAL: LIVING IN FANTASYLAND

Well, we've made it to Egypt, people, and now it's time to cross the river of denial. I like to conceptualize denial as equivalent

---

* Go get a highlighter and highlight this. Better yet, post this on social media so your online community knows what you now know. And yes, you can tell them I said so.

to living in fantasyland. It's radically accepting our present circumstances and then expecting transformation to magically take place. Or choosing to see our current reality as something completely different than it really is. It's like falling into the Chicago River, choosing to swim to shore, and expecting to step out onto to the white, warm sands of a Fiji beach. Ain't gonna happen. The one common characteristic that goes hand-in-hand with denial? Stubbornness. *Justification* is difficult to change because we fear invalidating our experiences. *Minimization* is a challenge because it involves actively choosing to lose something of importance in our lives. *Denial* is a pain in the butt because the first and only way to change this pattern of behavior is by changing our attitude to one of humility and receptivity. When my clients present with denial, I know we're in for the long haul.

There's only one key word that denial proclaims: "No." "No, that's not a problem." "No, that's not my responsibility." "No, I don't need to do that." "No, I don't need to change, you're the one who needs to change." See how much denial and stubbornness overlap? Another obstacle with denial is that we seek out ways to support our perspectives, what's referred to in psychology circles as "confirmation bias." Basically, it's our unconscious ability to look for and find information and situations that only support our evaluations, thereby driving our hold on their truth even deeper.

With justification, once you realize that changing your thoughts and actions doesn't mean excusing the mess others have dumped on your life, it becomes much easier to live your life moving in line with your values and purpose. So too with minimization. Here, you've already engaged the first step of seeing how YOU contribute to your current circumstances. Then, transformation occurs when you're willing to embrace the truth that loss is not only inevitable but will productively move you toward value-based and purpose-consistent decision-making.

Denial, on the other hand, requires a good, hard look in the mirror and the presence of safe, honest truth-tellers in your inner circle of community. We can only begin the process of shifting away from and out of denial when we choose to acknowledge that other possibilities *could* exist, and then open our mind and our heart to consideration of those possibilities. Notice I didn't say *acceptance*. One easy way to stay in denial is to approach change with an attitude that refuses even to entertain the idea, because you've decided it's impossible. It's like if you want to get from the North Rim of the Grand Canyon to the South Rim and you decide leaping over the Grand Canyon is the only way to get from here to there. With that kind of thinking you've quit before you even began, because the only options are true physical impossibilities. But if you really start thinking about it, you do have other choices, even though they might seem difficult at the time. Be open to those options.

FIGHTING FEAR

The most surefire way to do this is by recognizing the role fear plays in your resistance, adding fuel to your denial. I had a friend share with me not too long ago the pain of navigating her mother's end-of-life care at the hands of breast cancer. The hardest part for her, outside of watching her mom's ongoing physical suffering, was finding out that her mom knew about her condition a year before telling anyone, a year before she took active steps to treat it. She was afraid. Afraid of finding out how bad the prognosis might be, how painful and prolonged the treatment could be, and that she would burden and overwhelm her family with her growing needs and dependence. Unfortunately, fear motivated her to deny the reality of what came to ravage her body with sickness to the point that treatment was no longer possible.

The longer I practice, the more aware I am of the power we give fear in our lives.

Why do so many of us let fear stop us from taking that next step? As a therapist, one of the first things I do when working with a client is something called "case conceptualization." It's taking the client's history, their description of the presenting problem(s) they face, as well as contextual, situational, and relational factors, and creating a wholistic picture of what's really impacting their mental health and well-being, as well as what barriers need to be overcome for growth to occur. The longer I practice and the more I conceptualize, the more aware I am of the power we give fear in our lives and the overwhelming impact it has on many aspects of our day-to-day choices. In fact, I would go so far as to say that fear is one of the strongest motivators we encounter on a regular basis.

Unfortunately, the motivation we experience from fear is often the least productive when it comes to embracing who we are and what we can do. So how do we stop fear from being so debilitating? The first step is radically accepting fear will always be a part of your life. That doesn't mean you will **always** feel fear. It means that you'll never 100 percent escape fear. It is bound to spring up from time to time. However, embracing that reality means knowing how to react when fear rears its ugly head. Let's be honest: I've never heard someone say they were well prepared for a challenge because they avoided, denied, or minimized the obstacles standing in their way.

Next, picture what moving forward in *spite of your fear* would look like. Close your eyes, journal it out, do what you can to visualize a detailed picture of overcoming the fear. Finally, tell two of your people. You know, the people you trust to be your biggest cheerleaders and most honest critics. Ask them to listen without judgment—you're not looking for "that's a terrible idea" or even "you couldn't pick something better if you tried!" Ask them to listen with perspective, to consider your vision from a 360° angle and take into account as many variables as possible. Then have them provide two concrete steps that will set you on a course to punching fear in the face (aka, practical ways to achieve forward momentum).

Confronting denial is not going to obliterate the fear of potential outcomes. My friend's mom's fears all represented very feasible realities. The thing is, *they happened anyway*. She felt pain, the prognosis was not good, and her family did take on the burden of her care. Only, the outcome might have been different if she had been willing to consider a different approach to her fear; that embracing it by facing the prognosis, fighting the pain, and surrendering to the care could have resulted in her survival.

What if another option *could* exist—even if we fear the journey to get there? What would it take to consider that your actions *may be* communicating judgment, rejection, or worthlessness to others? How could you shift your perspective on how what you see and define as vital to your daily functioning *could* actually be more representative of conforming to the standards of Western culture and media-driven consumerism? What might open your mind to the option that your beliefs about a particular situation or circumstance might be based on ill-advised opinions instead of factual information? Here's the easiest step in the right direction I can offer you. Try swapping your "no" for a "maybe":

Denial: "No, that's not my problem."

Willingness: "Maybe part of this *is* my problem and I could contribute to the solution."

Denial: "No, that's not my responsibility."

Willingness: "Maybe I need to own some responsibility here."

Denial: "No, I don't need to do that."

Willingness: "Maybe I do need to do something different in order to move toward what's really important to me."

Denial: "No, I don't need to change, you're the one who needs to change."

Willingness: "Maybe I do need to change my approach for my own sake, even if the other person is unwilling to change."

Shifting from denial (stubbornness) to willingness is about saying YOU are worthy of experiencing and living aligned to your values and purpose no matter what others throw at you, even when it requires that you embrace uncomfortable decisions that you didn't choose to face in the first place. In fact, fighting the traps of justification and minimization are rooted in the same truth. It's hard work, but it is so rewarding in the long run.

• • •

HOW PURSUING COMMUNITY
IS LIKE REVERSING THE CHICAGO RIVER

One last thing worth mentioning as it relates to our ability and likelihood to change is the necessity of community in this process. Here's an interesting thought. As I mentioned above the flow of water typically moves in the direction of least resistance—usually. The direction of a river's flow actually shifts and changes based on its momentum. Like the adjustment in a river's current, the ability to shift and transform in our own lives requires momentum, something we can't always produce on our own. Did you know that the Chicago River actually flows "backward"? This was engineered in the late nineteenth century out of concern that the river's pollutants wouldn't overflow into Lake Michigan (where we get our drinking water. . . yum). This was a massive project, authorized in 1887 and completed in 1900. It took an entire team of civil engineers and construction workers to design and build a system of locks and increase the amount of Lake Michigan water coming into the river, thus forcing it to flow away from the lake.

So it is with the commitment to walk away from justification, minimization, and denial and to embrace the challenge of truly exploring and aligning yourself with your core values. You can't do it alone. Community is as critical to individual change as the increased energy of water is necessary to move an obstacle rather than go around it. If your life is missing the essential element of safe, supportive community, consider how you might make this your first action item on the list of embracing uncomfortable. If, right now, you're reacting with justification, minimization, or denial, go back and read this chapter with the need for community as your filter. I'm not saying this will be easy, quick, or convenient to put in place, but I am saying it will be essential.

My hope is this book will help both those who avoid *pursuing* community because of fears of rejection and those who avoid *providing* community because of fears of stepping beyond their zones of familiarity. We cannot do this alone, and we cannot accomplish these goals in the false safety of uniform spaces. Only among diversity of thought, culture, communication, and perspective can we confront the barriers to change outlined in this chapter and open the door to our truest selves.

9

CONQUERING THE "FAILURE" LIE . . . AND OTHER BATTLES

iden·ti·ty | \ ī-ˈden-tə-tē:
who you were created to be at your core before the
messiness of life tried to distort the image.

*What are the false beliefs about your core identity that prevent
from seeing the truth behind your overall purpose?*

I've done enough work as a counselor to see how consistently identity and purpose can become intertwined in unhealthy ways. When I first started writing this book, I polled a group of my close friends on this question: "What's something you really want to change in your life (something meaningful) but just haven't been able to? *Likely because of a lack of time or because it keeps getting shifted down on the list of priorities.*" We've built years of trust between us, so the responses were deep. Every one of them shared something that is consistent with what I've struggled with and what I know others default to more often than they want to. Here are a few highlights:

• • •

"*Walking and living out who I know I am and not reverting back to the lies I used to believe about me: I'm a weirdo. God made me wrong. I'm too much, too loud, and too sensitive. You are all going to stop being my friends.*"

"*I would love to change my lack of confidence. I always believe the lie that I am a fraud at everything I do. I feel like a fraud as a mom, a wife, [at] work, leading a Bible study, you name it. I feel like I am incompetent. While I know this is not how God has equipped me or made me, I still believe it most days.*"

"*Sometimes I just want to be me. The old me, a new me, someone that's not responsible for someone else other than myself. Because if that was the case then I wouldn't feel selfish when I do something for myself or miss something about my precious life or think about all the thousands of things I want to do with my life but can't because I'm a mom. Then my mind moves into the question of 'why can't I do those things even though I am a mom?' Other people seem to do it all, have it all together, and I can't. I know in my head it's probably not perfect for them either—anyone can pose and decorate and shop at the right place to make their life look A-OK—but it still messes with me.*"

"*I avoid putting my work into the world because, on the surface, I fear the unknown but under that is a lack of trust in myself. I fear that I cannot show up consistently for the people who begin to depend on me and if I fail them, they will abandon me. Ultimately, I don't step into my fullest potential because I'm convinced I'm a failure before I even begin.*"

FAILURE AS AN IDENTITY

"I'm a failure before I even begin." Fear of failure was evident in every response I received from my closest inner circle of community. The dreaded F word. It's interesting how we can turn words into nouns. This word *failure* first connoted a deficiency, to be lacking, not succeed. It was later, like two hundred years later, that we turned it into a sense of *being*—an identity. While it may have been wrapped in different packaging for each one of my friends, the root roadblock was consistently the same. Fear was the emotion and failure was the outcome each was desperately trying to avoid.

However, if you dig a bit deeper there's a greater deception well beneath the surface. Yes, avoiding failure was the motivation keeping each of my friends from stepping into uncomfortable spaces, but the hard truth was that each of them (and I would argue each of *us*) had allowed failure to transform from an action to an identity. Yes, they feared failure, but more than that they feared being seen or identifying themselves *as* failures. After all, I might be okay failing behind closed doors. I'm okay pressing Control-Alt-Delete as long as no one's looking. What stops me in my tracks is this

> They feared failure, but more than that they feared being seen as failures.

overwhelming pressure of others' grip on me and how they will treat me as they see me failing, or more importantly, how they will treat me after I fail.

This is so reflective of our society. We've allowed failure to become this unspeakable disaster that must be avoided at all costs, because the outcome is more than we can handle or even survive. When did failure become one's whole identity instead of the reality of what it stands for, a lack of success?* I can tell you right now, I've *not* succeeded in a lot of things (if you need a refresher on this, please read chapter 1), and I'm going to continue to do so. If I place my ability to embrace uncomfortable on the guarantee of success, I might as well add this failure to the heaping mound of others crowding my life's backyard.

In order to live out our values and pursue our purpose by intentionally embracing uncomfortable, we HAVE TO change the narrative around failure and radically accept it will be a part of our lives but is not a description of our identity. A good story is never without conflict, without a struggle and obstacles to overcome. Imagine if we went to movies where the storyline was all rainbows and unicorns from beginning to end. Refund please. No, the story you will tell is the blockbuster trilogy that your life is, alive with the calls to adventure beyond your comfort zone and into action-packed conflict that turns you into the hero you have been waiting for since you were five. Choosing to take the risk is the page-turner moment you need to give yourself permission to seize.

Let me set you up for realistic expectations. This is a difficult ongoing task that cannot be accomplished without intentionality and a willingness to take risks. Yet even this "take risks" mantra, when it comes from others, just comes off judgmental, not encouraging. The millionaire will tell the poor person, "Take risks and one day you'll fulfill your purpose *and* your bank account!" Yeah, okay. Your pushy confidence makes others recoil. No, let's keep risk-taking within the boundaries where it belongs. A willingness to take a risk is simply saying "I'm afraid, and I'm going to

---

* Perfect place for a purposeful pause. When and how did failure become an identity in your life? When did your identity become weighed by the number of zeros on your paycheck or the number of followers on your social media? When did someone's stamp of approval become the seal of approval on your life?

step into it afraid." That's taking life by the boldness and showing up with all the lack of confidence your confidence can afford. And in that moment, for that day, that was enough. It is possible, and I know this firsthand.

I would go against my very value of authenticity if I didn't share with you my experiences of wrestling with the false identity of failure. While we all face the mini-trials that can instigate minor to moderate encounters with failure, I can share three experiences that fueled the flames of a failure identity in big ways in my life story. One was the experience of concrete failure seven times over on that comprehensive exam. Each government-sealed, stamped letter I received with the words "did not pass" spurred a wave of self-judgment and criticism regarding my intellect, my ability to ingest the knowledge of psychology, and my overall capabilities as a student. I was waiting for a stamp of approval and when I didn't get it, the results of my exam became a seal of approval on my life. Deep down, the fears of how my colleagues and professors viewed me (incompetent, a fraud, lacking self-awareness) and how clearly deceived I was in thinking I could become a skilled psychologist were the demons overshadowing an identity grounded in who I was not what I did. Once I did pass that exam, the fear had already taken root and I was driven to succeed because I thought I was fighting to avoid the failure of inadequacy. Thankfully (and painfully), some hard work in therapy and a considerable amount of self-reflection helped unearth this deeper fear of failure in my life.

"YOU WEREN'T MEANT TO BE HERE"

As I mentioned earlier, the start of my life story is the experience of adoption. While I can confidently say now this is an illustration in my story, for many years I struggled with it being the title of the book. Adoption as an identity meant that regardless of how loved I was and have been by my parents, there was always a voice that constantly whispered in the back of my head: *you weren't meant to be here.* Remember that lie I wrestled with, the polarity of being chosen because I came from a place of being let go? It drove my choices as I feared failing to be seen and experienced as *necessary* . . . wanted. I feared ultimately becoming an expendable burden.

Isn't that the longing deep inside all of our hearts? The desire to belong—to truly belong. I think sometimes we feel like this even when we are chosen. We fear that just as I have been chosen, I could also easily be unchosen, because those who love me will always love themselves more.

When did this start happening in our storylines? We live out myths in a very real world, and we desperately hope that they are false but (not so secretly) believe they are oh so terrifyingly real. I have fought long and hard against the lie that told me I had to earn my place in order to be significant and worth keeping around.

Community is a powerful tool for working through misplaced identity, and I've had amazing people speak truth against the lies I battle. Still, this process is hard, and I can say both personally and professionally that it's never fully complete. We hike mountains and then trudge through valleys in the work of shedding false beliefs about who we are and the fears that motivate us into unhealthy decisions.

WHEN I WASN'T "ENOUGH"

My third experience in my wrestling with fear of failure and the false identity of worthlessness has carried the most crushing weight on my journey and likes to silently hide in wait to attack when I am unguarded and vulnerable.

To wrestle with one lie that a mother has intentionally left you is tough. To wrestle with two tangible (albeit false) experiences of failing to be enough can come close to destruction. When my mom took her life, it was a catastrophic loss for so many. Her pain ran deep, and I couldn't begin to know the lies she was wrestling with herself. Yet I also cannot deny the marker this choice has left on my life and my struggle with fearing the failure of being enough, enough to keep and find worthy of belonging. This deceptive identity tries to hold me back from pushing forward, climbing mountains, and pursuing my purpose. It fights hard to convince me of the message that I'm not enough and I shouldn't be in the room. When our focal point is tightly set on our "failure," it becomes the lens through which we see and interpret the world around us. It becomes the potential for all outcomes and then serves as the foundation for the fear wall we build in defense of avoidance.

The only way out is to take off the glasses and recognize that experiences create meaning, not measure. Losing my mom is not a measure of my worth any more than failing that test or being released from the bond of a biological parent is. The beautiful thing I've come to realize is that I can navigate the pain of those messages from an emotional standpoint, but they will never conquer my identity and the total lie that they can define me.

"THIS HAPPENED, AND THIS IS HOW I FEEL ABOUT IT"

I've already shared with you the importance of balancing our emotions and our rational understanding and interpretation of our circumstances, but there's a critical step in that process many of us miss. If you remember from chapter 6, radical acceptance is like a good old-fashioned Venn diagram that says, "Fact: this happened to me in this circle over here." We call it rationality. It's black and white, logical, tangible, real. It's without judgment—not good or bad, it just is. Then radical acceptance says, "I have emotions related to this experience in this circle over *here*. I feel angry, I feel bitter, I feel hurt, I feel ashamed; I feel unworthy." Like your rational thoughts and experiences, your emotional thoughts and experiences *just are*. They are not good or bad, right or wrong, they simply exist in the moment. However, before you determine what is rational and what is emotional, you have to have a solid foundational understanding of *who you are,* and that's the biggest step we struggle to both initiate and practice on a regular basis.

What happens most often is we allow our experiences and our emotions to define us instead of holding them within the boundaries of things that have happened to us. This is where I was trapped.

Experience: Couldn't pass my comprehensive exam

Feeling: Disappointment, rejection, inadequacy

Identity: Failure

Experience: Biological mom chose to give me up versus keeping me

Feeling: Disappointment, rejection, inadequacy

Identity: Failure

Experience: Adopted mom chose death over life

Feeling: Disappointment, rejection, inadequacy

Identity: Failure (see the pattern?)

I was in a vicious cycle that derailed my ability to pursue purpose because I felt unworthy, and that kept me from seeing myself as capable. One by one as I tore down the manipulative messages trying to rob my sense of self, I came to see that these experiences didn't define me. Held within the boundaries of emotions and circumstances, they impacted me, no doubt, but they didn't steal me from the opportunity to show what was really my core identity as highlighted through the living out of my values and purpose. In that space, I could hold both the knowledge that I was going to be in places where I made mistakes, wasn't fully capable, would let others down (and they in turn would likely do the same to me). Both these things would lead to feelings of disappointment, anger, shame, guilt, rejection, or frustration. However, that did not mean my identity was worthlessness, that failure defined me, or that I wasn't still living out my purpose. That's how I was able to move forward. I took radical acceptance with me every step of the way. Radical thought said, "I may not be equipped (I don't have the resources, the knowledge, the experience)"; emotional thought said, "I'm afraid." Identity and purpose said, "Move anyway because that equipping and that fear don't define you."

IT *WILL* HAPPEN—SO WHAT WILL YOU DO THEN?

So, I'm on a campaign to recapture our approach to failure and I'm charging us to start from the point that *it will happen.* So, instead of avoiding it, think about how you're going to powerfully plow through it and who you're going to be when you do. One of my most memorable experiences over the last five years was the Cubs winning the World Series. I'll never forget that night and the way Chicago erupted in celebration over the team whose motto had come to be "Try Not to Suck." It's easy to argue the Cubs have encountered their fair share of failures, even throughout that amazing, memorable 2016 season. Yet we don't define their championship by that. In fact, could you imagine buying a limited-edition baseball cap that read "58 losses this season" in addition to "World Series Champs"?

Let's stop limiting ourselves by the question, "What if I (or they) experience the consequences of my failure?" and instead start asking ourselves, who do we want to be in the midst of a failure? I recently had a client who wanted to improve the way he engaged in the various roles in his life. He wanted to be a better boss, and a better spouse, and a better father. He was also trapped by the narrative of a failure identity. He desperately feared letting others down and so he narrowed the playing field by choosing to believe he was never really capable to begin with. The identity he was choosing to embrace was "However hard I try I'll never be good enough," and his view through those skewed tinted lenses reinforced this belief. This not only gave him permission to unconsciously seek out ongoing opportunities for failure (self-fulfilling prophecy) but reinforced this identity by holding him hostage to the narrative he'd constructed based on his past experiences and internalized beliefs about his worth and consequently how he defined who he was. How do you embrace uncomfortable to pursue purpose and values when your foundation is the sinking quicksand of self-defeat? Remember, you're the protagonist of your narrative, not the antagonist. Step into your role. I mean, who else is going to play you?

Failure is something to expect, not something to absorb.

So, together we worked to define his core purpose: *be present and engaged in my relationships to recognize the innate value inherent in others* (he's really smart). Then we began to shift his perspective on failure: it was something to expect but not something to absorb. When a failure presented itself, he shifted to first asking the question "What happened?" and responding, "I made a mistake, I feel disappointed." Then he returned to his purpose. "Am I still able to shift in my posture and presence to be engaged in this relationship as a reflection of my understanding of this individual's value?" The answer was always yes, because the only roadblock was the unwillingness to embrace uncomfortable, not a fear wall of failure.

Now, I'm making this sound like the shift happened overnight. It didn't. We worked together for several years before this became an intentional part of his daily routine, but the point is he released failure from his identity! He said "bye!" to the all-or-nothing perspective that letting others down or that experience in return was the end to his story. He learned to be honest and accept responsibility for his actions because defending his position was no longer required when it ceased to define his identity. Over time, this turned into consistency, which also happens to be the most powerful communication tool because it builds a foundation of trust. As his relationships transformed, the reinforcement of a fulfilled purpose drove his desire to live according to his values.

Here's the deal: at some point or another, we are going to let people down and they are going to experience the consequences of our failures. So what if they do? Does that eliminate the consequences they experience from our successes? Is it an all-or-nothing situation? Absolutely not.

Listen, for all I know it is just you and I thumbing through this book. My publisher might see it as a failure. I choose to see it as a complete win. I wrote a book. You read a book. Win win. And so here we are, let's change the narrative. You can't drop the mic if the mic isn't in your hands. Stop letting failure dictate the outcome of your storyline, story circle, square ... you get it. Step out into it. Take the risk. What's the worst that can happen? You'll have a great story to tell! And when you tell it narrate every word like you lived it.

Authentically yours,

Dr. (finally) Deb

THE CLOSING CHAPTER—KEEP THE DOOR OPEN

em·brace | \ im-ˈbrās un·com·fort·able | \ ˈən-ˈkəm(p)(f)-tər-bəl:
the ultimate goal of this book.

What's stopping you now?

Six years ago, I was living in this artist-type loft apartment with my best friend, Patty. We hadn't been living there long and decided to throw a party with some of our friends to show off the new place. Always hovering on the edge of naivete, I decided to leave our front door unlocked because it was the dead of February winter and nobody wanted to traipse up and down the stairs to the chill of ten degrees as they were arriving. What could even possibly go wrong with leaving your door unlocked in the heart of a major city like Chicago?

Just slightly before 7 p.m. we heard the door open. Several people were coming up the entryway. Expecting a few of our early-arriving friends (you know the type), we were quite surprised to see six strangers walk into our living room. Here's the thing: perhaps two normal people would have immediately panicked, attempted to bum-rush them out the door, or called the cops. However, Patty and I looked at this small group of women and simply assumed they were friends of friends we hadn't met yet and who were invited to the join the party via grapevine. As we offered to take their coats and asked if they'd like something to drink, we both apparently brushed off any hint of discomfort in the vibes they were giving off. We both shrugged, thinking they were just uncomfortable arriving before their friends to a stranger's house. Small talk ensued, and it didn't take too long to realize something was amiss. Two women refused (kindly but repeatedly) to take off their coats despite the constant flow of a nice warm heater, and just stiffly stood near the entryway. Two other women started wandering around looking at the sparse artwork that covered just one or two of our walls. However, the remaining two women made themselves right at home, diving into our snacks and animatedly talking about the unique layout of the apartment. With frequent questioning glances, we attempted to go with this peculiar flow of events, until someone asked which one of us was the artist.

Come to find out, Patty and I had moved into an artist community and our new apartment was located smack-dab in the middle of a monthly art walk. We knew the place below us had been a studio at some point (and was now just an empty "for rent" space filled with a bunch of fake trees that gave off the illusion we were living above what seemed like a dying forest), but we had no idea the entire neighborhood was mostly artists and the four-block radius around where we lived offered an open house the third Friday of every month. These six women, who were now scrambling to grab their coats and apologizing for walking right into our house, had merely thought we were another stop on the tour! As we laughed and tried to assure them the mistake was natural given I had LEFT THE DOOR OPEN, five more strangers walked up the stairs (because when you walk into the home of a stranger who's left their door unlocked, you don't just naturally then lock it behind you). In the chaos of eleven strangers now trying to determine if they should stay or go, several of our friends finally arrived, only to let four more strangers into the house assuming we knew them and THEY just hadn't met yet!

What possessed us to shrug our shoulders and go with the flow that night, I'll never really understand. All I know is by the time the night was over, we'd had over eighty strangers in our home, eating our food, drinking our drinks, playing our games, and creating the most memorable evening of laughter, conversation, and sheer absurdity over two women who would bravely open their door to a crowd of strangers on a freezing Chicago night. The next morning, we sat in the kitchen in disbelief over the entire experience, equal parts still a bit shocked but also quite amused at this ridiculous memory we'd just made (and relieved that everything was still in its place and the house wasn't trashed). For the friends who weren't there, the next several weeks presented the opportunity to share this crazy story of leaving the door open and letting a bunch of strangers into our home.

Then another third Friday rolled around and we both happened to be home when there was a knock at our door. Those first six women were back (sans one) and wanted to know if we planned to host again.

COME ON IN!

I don't know about you, but the idea of letting an unpredictable number of unknown visitors into my home on a monthly basis was the last thing I would ever see myself doing. I'm the Type A personality that wants everything in its place and every speck dusted away before I even let my closest friends come over for dinner. I'm also the friend most likely to fall asleep on the couch at 9 p.m. on a Friday night after a long week at work. However, I couldn't shake two thoughts the night those women asked if we planned to host again—my value of relationship and my purpose of building community by embracing uncomfortable. (As a side note, do everything you can to find a best friend who shares similar values or compliments them with great joy. Patty values community and creating space for people to feel welcomed, cared for, and encouraged.) Over the

> What can we do to embrace the uncomfortable and what might be the outcome if we're willing to step into that space?

next two years, we committed to stepping into the uncomfortable and opening our home almost every third Friday to whoever was out strolling the art walk that night. We built community with neighbors, strangers, and visitors from all over the world. We experienced impromptu monologues from a group of local actors, a jazz performance from two guys lugging around tubas, and carried on the most bizarre conversation I've ever had with one guy who claimed to be an alien transported to this current date and time from a place two thousand years into the future. We also made friends, knew who to borrow sugar from on Thanksgiving morning when the stores were closed, and would be randomly asked by a waitress in a restaurant across town if we were the two roommates who opened their door and let people into their home during the Third Friday art walks because she was quite sure she'd been in our house.

I share this story because we've come to the close of our time together and I want to end with an illustration of expectations. What can we do to embrace the uncomfortable and what might be the outcome if we're willing to step into that space? And what is really the greatest barrier that prevents us from going there? Never in a million years would I think that the beginning of my journey in stepping into uncomfortable spaces would start with building relationships with hundreds of strangers who set foot in my home over the course of a few years. However, in retrospect, that was merely the catalyst for recognizing the impact of embracing uncomfortable and what I could experience in life if I made a commitment to being open to opportunities I might never consider otherwise. Uncomfortable had been a part of my DNA for a while. I was now able to see it with a fresh perspective and commitment to intentionally pursuing it. I was also able to see how fear could truly be overcome in the process.

Let me pause here for a moment and clarify that last remark. It's not an uncommon phrase, "overcome your fears," but I do believe it is a misunderstood one. I think we have this unconscious belief that "overcoming fear" means we do the action we're afraid of when we no longer fear the fear. So we wait for the fear to subside before we engage in whatever activity we're afraid of. That's basically the same thing as me saying, "I'll start going to the gym regularly when I feel excited and enthusiastic about working out." Ain't gonna happen. However, I CAN go to the gym even if I dread it. Just like I can step toward the things I'm afraid of even if I feel terrified at the thought of that or the potential failures that could result (we're rarely afraid of the successes).

I realize that for many of you the thought (and safety) of letting complete strangers into your home sounds just terrible. That's fair. The point of my story isn't to encourage you to make some outlandish decision in the name of embracing uncomfortable. I don't want you to place yourself in danger or set out *just to prove a point*. I also don't want you to mimic my example; the goal is to consider your unique personality, circumstances, and YOUR values and purpose. Then the challenge is to consider where you might be closing the door on an opportunity simply because it doesn't fall into your norm, because it makes you feel too uncomfortable.

BEING INTENTIONAL—EVERY DAY

As I've said throughout this book, the only way to actively and fully engage this process is through a discipline of intentionality. I may not have intentionally left the door open that night in February winter, but I intentionally chose to leave the door open every third Friday thereafter. We have to commit to purposeful, thoughtful reflection on our daily decisions if we hope to align with our values and purpose. This is simply a non-negotiable. As we add more to our plates and less to our purpose, we lose who we are and the powerful monsters of justification, minimization, and denial drive us forward into the crowd of conformity. I once read a powerful statement that continues to influence my approach to embracing uncomfortable to this day, "Don't become so well-adjusted to your culture that you fit into it without even thinking."

Stop adjusting yourself to the temporary comforts of life at the expense of what you value most. Stop waking up each morning and flipping on autopilot. Stop allowing the excuses of things you've miscategorized as impossibilities prevent you from living out who you've been purposed to be. Finally, make a commitment to step out of the trap of others' behaviors sinking you in the quicksand of a place you didn't choose and a circumstance you don't like or want. Choose to seek community in this process. Choose to seek support. Choose to choose (because we can easily live life by the choices made by others). Recognize that roadblocks, obstacles, mistakes, and reroutes will happen at every step of this journey, and no one ever said you couldn't pause and reorient yourself before getting back behind the wheel. Be your own bus driver Betty. Be willing to take ownership and responsibility over *what is yours*. Embracing uncomfortable requires a daily dose of humility. Do a gut check when humility seems out of reach or unnecessary. (Spoiler alert: humility doesn't equal submissiveness or a lack of confidence—it's a posture of listening to understand even if you aren't afforded that response in return.) Humility also says you can shake the dust from your shoes and walk away—just consider how you communicate dissolving a partnership and how you'll react if reconciliation is presented in the future.

> As we add more to our plates and less to our purpose, we lose who we are.

In the grand scheme of my life experiences, opening the door was actually one of the easiest of decisions among a multitude of decisions made in the span of my lifetime. Sure, it required some discomfort and a loss of the occasional Friday-night chill fest. Yes, I had to embrace the loss of controlling how my house looked when that first stranger walked up the steps, or the hours of small talk I had to engage in that are the antithesis of this introvert, one-on-one relator's preferences. Yet, the stretching that was produced from choosing to step into the uncomfortable of the unknowns that made up those amazing Friday night art walks was more of a primer for the things in my life that have been much more painful. Now, when I think of the art walk, I think of it like my dry run or the easy metaphor whose message applies to the more difficult journeys in life. And that's how I want to leave the door open for you—with the challenging application of embracing uncomfortable and not the easier, just-slide-by opportunities that might make you squirm a bit but ultimately ease you right back in to the habitual choices of everyday living.

HOLDING TIGHT TO THE BLAMING

Since I began this journey with you by sharing about my love story with Chicago, I thought I'd end with the reality of my transition here, which was not an easy one. I came here knowing very few people and having minimal connections. In August 2012, I moved to Chicago to work for a nonprofit organization doing leadership consulting and organizational psychology. In my first few months in the city, my priority was to learn the culture, dynamic, and needs of my new workplace and to get involved in a local church. Between August and December, I had accomplished both goals. Unfortunately, the "learning the culture, dynamic, and needs of my workplace" goal led to the "this is not the job I signed up for" epiphany. By spring 2013, I was quickly becoming aware of the reality that my new position would not last, and the funds in my bank account took on a whole different level of importance as I was slowly transitioned out of what I thought would be a salaried position, to an hourly part-time role, and was eventually told I would be "contracted as needed"—which ultimately led to just being "ghosted."

It was like a bad breakup. Just shy of my one-year anniversary of living in Chicago, I was out of a job and more importantly, out of direction. My choices were bleak and nearly all pointed to the likelihood of moving out of a city I had quickly grown to love and call home.

I don't know if you've walked a season of "nos," a season when you seem to be stripped away of all that you've built or hoped to accomplish. But this was my second journey through the deep pain of heavy loss. I felt angry, I felt hurt. I felt justified in a lot of harsh words and bitter thoughts. I found comfort in a place of defensiveness, blaming, and justification. For me, this is the hardest place to push into uncomfortable—when my actions feel justified. And after years of counseling, coaching, observing leaders, colleagues, and friends, and engaging in conversation after conversation with people stuck in the painful cycle of being hurt by others, I have seen enough examples of this reactive response to know that justification ranks number one as the biggest barrier to embracing uncomfortable. Even when justification is justified.

It's as if we get stuck in this place of fear that letting go of the wrongs means we're no longer right. So we hold tight to the blaming at the loss of moving on, and the consequence is too often our misery. We justify our actions misaligning with our values and we justify our unwillingness to engage with our purpose. Our perspective ruminates on revenge or the injustice of it all, and we fail to lose sight of the direction it takes us . . . far into the wilderness of lost opportunities.

I stayed in that place for a long time. Even after I'd found the beginnings of the amazing job I have now, and my finances started to slowly climb back into the black. Even after I'd signed a lease on that creative, open-space loft above the dead tree forest, a loft that would later open the door to a bunch of strangers who would eventually become the foundation for some of my most influential memories. Even after I'd built a strong community and started to fall in love with this city I would come to easily call home.

I brooded and I blamed, yet nothing was enough. As the saying goes, "hurt people hurt people." I was hurt by a hurt person, and in my pain, I was hoping for the hurt to continue as I passed it on to others.

One thing I always tell my clients early on in counseling is that we'll never solve the problem of what others have done to them, hurting them, inflicting pain and anger. I also acknowledge the reality that we'll never eliminate the opposite, either—*our* ability to cause hurt and anger in others. What we will always have power over is our response.

> We will never eliminate the pain others inflict on us or the pain we bring on others. What we will always have power over is our response.

When I went through my job loss, I defended my thoughts of being betrayed, viewing my current circumstances (out of a job, selling my car, unable to afford my rent, losing my health insurance) through the lens of bitterness and being dealt with unfairly. The truth is, I *was* treated dishonestly, and the consequences were broad and long lasting, but this was not my endgame.

Remember, the beauty of uncomfortable is it's also a marker for us to reevaluate. I took a long, hard look at my values and core purpose and started to list the ways my actions, *regardless* of my circumstances and whether or not I chose to be here, were aligning and misaligning with what mattered most to me. And what mattered most to me? Jesus, relationship, wisdom, authenticity, purpose. But I didn't see Jesus in my actions. I was using my relationships for justification. Wisdom had turned to rationalization. My thoughts and behavior were inauthentic to my core and my purpose was lost in the process.

One by one I began to retrace my steps back to the authentic me. When a bitter thought or a motivation to ruminate on my unchosen circumstances presented itself, I acknowledged the pain. I *was* hurt, I *felt* angry, and I had been *treated* unfairly, but these experiences did not change the fact that I still wanted to meet people in their pain, build bridges of transformational community in my city, and challenge others to actively live more consistent to their beliefs through leading by example. When I validated the pain and committed to pushing into uncomfortable places, I experienced greater authenticity and contentment in my choices and my direction. The catch was, I could only go so far in doing this on my own. I needed community to push me forward when the barriers were too steep to climb solo.

THE GARDEN OF COMMUNITY

Unfortunately, I think the value of community has taken a significant hit in the majority-culture, Western ideological mindset. All too often I hear the words "I'm too busy, I have too much going on, I don't have time" in response to the various calls for community. In his book *Tribes*, author Seth Godin states, "Human beings can't help it: we need to belong. One of the most powerful of our survival mechanisms is to be part of a tribe, to contribute to (and take from) a group of like-minded people."[1] Yet when I look at my clients and the challenges they struggle with, too often the underlying source is the absence of true, honest, sustainable community in their daily lives—because the people around them have too much going on. We fill our buckets until they are overflowing with commitments and expectations that are so beyond our values and desires, but we don't have the capacity for intentionality, so we just continue to react to the daily decisions coming at us. And what seems to be the first casualty of a reactive culture is a community of intimate, purposeful, prioritized connection.

Do you know what births out of a lack of intentionality? Unhealthy habits. Think about it. No once chooses an addiction. Addiction stems from an unmindful choice (one that fails to consider values, consequence, and impact) that slowly becomes a pattern of behavior that is eventually incredibly difficult to break. I am saying that if you don't practice the discipline of consideration, all the things that want to pull you away from investment in community will gradually become habit. So, in my season of process and growth, it was critical that I add community as a priority in order to persevere through.

Community has become my sustenance, but it has also been a garden I've had to cultivate slowly, with purpose and patience. The pursuit of community has been its own exercise in embracing uncomfortable and continues to be a place that pushes (and pulls and drags) me toward that squirming place of reflection, re-centering, and ultimately growth. I have to honestly say that I'm in love with this season of life. The uncomfortable is both individually and mutually experienced. My experience matters. Your experience matters. WE matter. And that's what this moment on a cold, February night in the heart of Chicago was all about.

A door left open.

A group of women who chose to step out of the cold and into a home.

These women then chose to stay.

They were uncomfortable.

We were uncomfortable.

COMFORT, CHALLENGE, AND COMMUNITY

It was when we found common ground that an unintended moment was transformed into an intentional circumstance to create space for others to find comfort in an uncomfortable space. These are the spaces that bring healing, growth, connection, and the opportunity to face our fears in order to authentically pursue our purpose.

To that end, my challenge to you, as you come to an understanding of the critical role of embracing uncomfortable in living authentic to your values and purpose, is to make a commitment to pursue a community you can look to and learn from. Consider building a community that prioritizes relationships embedded within a collective focus. While independence has its values, our relationships in support of and with others, characteristics of selflessness and humility, and the truth that our identity is fundamentally connected to others is deeply attached to the development of our values and purpose.

For me, engaging an honest evaluation of my purpose and values has meant challenging my Western cultural mindset that leans toward the values of distinctiveness, autonomy, and a developing independence from others, and shifting toward the influence of my brothers and sisters whose cultures place significant worth in family, social relationships, dependence, humility, generosity, the pursuit of unity, and acts of selflessness.

What I find most interesting is the way in which we describe ourselves based on being immersed in an individualistic culture versus a collectivistic one. Cross-cultural psychologists[1] have found that people from individualistic cultures typically describe themselves in what is referred to as "nonsocial" terms, explaining their personalities and skill sets from a self-focused perspective, "I am smart, funny, athletic, and kind." In contrast, those from collectivistic cultures are more inclined to use interdependent or social terms, highlighting their social relationships and roles, "I am a good son/daughter, brother/sister, and friend." I don't know about you—but I would rather those that knew me describe me as the latter.

Make no mistake: a commitment to community will require an embracing of sacrifice. Remember, every decision we make involves a loss! Consider the loss you want to avoid and the gain you want to pursue. To fully engage embracing uncomfortable, community has to be your bedrock. To that end, I want to be for you who my community has been for me.

I recognize that building community can be hard. Finding the people who listen to understand, support with critical and insightful questions, speak truth with equal parts grace and resolve, and are willing to go with you into the tough, sensitive, vulnerable places in your life is not an overnight task. Yet it's only in that type of community—where you can return to a space where you are known to your core—can you really filter out the stuff clogging the view of your North Star. A space where people remind you who you are and allow the raw emotions of painful life without judgment or dismissal. It's this type of community that's created opportunities for me to see when I'm valuing relationship and when it's taken a backseat to misplaced priorities. My community has encouraged and listened as I've processed heavy emotions, which allowed me to see what was truth in my life and where feelings were influencing my perspectives in misguided ways. For me, it's nearly impossible to function inauthentically within a community that knows your motivations, your personality, your strengths and weaknesses, and your values. Community is my accountability.

So, for those of you still searching for your own safe circles to launch from into the practice of embracing uncomfortable or for those needing some extra support, we've created an online space (embracinguncomfortable.com) to encourage, listen, and inspire you to places of uncomfortable growth. We'll share together the challenges and celebrate the hard work and success of leaning into the patient, intentional practice of pursuing our values and purpose in all areas of our lives. Together we will champion transformation in our relationships, our workspaces, our everyday interactions, and our communities. I wrote this book because I believe a willingness to embrace uncomfortable can ignite a revolution where people overcome the barriers blocking them from becoming today who they've always been and were created to be. Thank you for gifting me space in your life to light the flame or blow on the already burning embers. I am excited to continue on this journey from wherever you are, in whatever circumstance you may be in—slowing down at speed bumps or trying to hurl yourself over walls. We can step out together as we push one another toward the daily practice of embracing uncomfortable.

Afterword

STILL SITTING UP!

I'll never forget the first time one of my clients told me, "You must really have it all together to do the kind of work you do." My first thought was, "Yes, I fooled him!" No, the real answer is that I panicked inside. My thoughts spiraled into a tornado of self-doubt ("I DEFINITELY don't have it all together—should I go back to wrangling celebrities? At least I'll be in good company there!") and then defensiveness ("Not one person in my graduate program told me a prerequisite to be a psychologist is to have it all together! I want my money back.").

Thankfully, I've learned a little something (not all the somethings . . . but a few of the somethings) since my infancy in this profession and the blessed naïveté of my well-meaning client. We're all on the same playing field. In our counseling education program, we are very intentional to steer clear of and challenge the use of the word "fix." Mental health professionals are not in the business of fixing people; we're gifted the opportunity to step into personal, vulnerable spaces at the invitation of our clients to journey alongside them.

When I told friends and family I was writing a book about

embracing uncomfortable, it became the running joke to challenge my practice of this concept when I shared with them the frustrations, missteps, and challenges of my daily life. It wasn't done in malice or defense; it was good-natured humor and occasional challenges to accountability because the people in my inner circle know that I'm just as broken as the next woman or man. Embracing uncomfortable is just as hard for me as it is for those that have shared their efforts to step into similar spaces. My hope and prayer is that this has been evident throughout the book so that maybe you were able to experience a tiny taste of validation and a pinch of hope that you **can do this**!

I want to leave you with one last story. God has a funny way of taking me to the "just abouts" in life and then leaving me dangling there for a bit (honestly, what feels like forever). After practicing as a psychologist in the typical see-clients-on-the-hour fashion for several years after graduating, I decided that I wasn't built to be the average talk therapist. Instead, I was convinced my true calling was as a hostage negotiator. I applied for and was initially greenlighted for screening into the field agent program of the FBI. I passed weeks of interviews, a polygraph test, and a written exam designed to ensure I wasn't insane. Then came the physical fitness assessment. In my early thirties, I was in fairly good shape but no Ninja Warrior, so I hit the gym, partnered up with another applicant for accountability, and started pushing myself in preparation. When the day came for my evaluation, I was certain I was ready. Sit-ups—check. Three-quarter sprint—check. Push-ups—barely check. One point-five-mile run—check. Exhausted, my fellow applicants and I sat on the ground, fighting to catch our breath as the points of our performance (number of, form, and time) were tallied.

I missed the cutoff by one sit-up that didn't break a ninety-degree angle.

All the fears of all the "failures" I'd seen myself stumbling over in life came rushing to the front of my mind. I limped from the field to my car with tears streaming down my face. Not even the question of *why* managed to flash across my mind. Instead, all I could think of was "sounds about right." One simple thought obliterated a much greater and impactful perspective: every sit-up that DID break ninety degrees! That I managed to sprint, SPRINT (if you've never tried sprinting—well, it's terrible) 300 meters around a track in forty-five seconds! That I was still standing! Instead, I allowed my identity and my worth to be summed up in defeat.

That's what we do. We struggle to see what's there because we're hyper-focused on what's missing. Yet there's always going to be the one missed sit-up in my life. The one-point-shy-of-passing-the-exam experience. Those experiences are going to be just as present in each of our lives as the "I-got-the-armoire-up-the-freakin'-stairs" accomplishments.

I wrote this book to remind myself that every day I have the opportunity to choose embracing uncomfortable or defaulting to comfort. Some days I'll succeed, and many days I won't. Some days I'll succeed and still feel disappointment, and some days I'll fail and be able to shrug it off and commit to trying again; other days I'll fail and spiral into a temporary state of self-doubt and fear. However, if I'm willing, if you're willing, we can see the missed sit-up, mourn the meaning of its loss, and choose to shift our perspective to the truth that even 80 degrees, 50 degrees, heck . . . even .0001 degrees is still *sitting up*.

ACKNOWLEDGMENTS

People say raising a child takes a village. In my experience, surviving life takes a village (so does writing a book). I am honored to thank the following people for trekking this journey with me (as if they had a choice).

Dad, thank you for instilling in me the value of connection and the passion for investigating the puzzles of human behavior. It's because of your legacy that I'm driven to seek out perspectives that bring people together instead of driving them apart, whether in the counseling office, the classroom, in line at the movies, or riding in an Uber. I can hardly wait for our next walk through the streets of Chicago.

Sis and Carter, you are the best answer to the most important question I've ever asked in my life: "God, will you PLEASE give me a sister and a brother??" Thank you for having my back no matter what (and, let's be honest, making me uncomfortable . . . A LOT).

Every time you, my dear reader, laughed in this book a middle-school teacher named Patty gained an ounce of energy to serve the rambunctious seventh graders she ministers to every day. P, this book wouldn't have happened without you. You pushed me through temper tantrums, helped add flavor to my stories, and patiently read and reread every chapter to assure me I wasn't crazy and what I was writing actually did make sense. Thanks for being my best friend! I solemnly swear to uphold our napkin contract and never make you move another large piece of furniture with me ever again.

To my Sassy Sisters: We survived the awkwardness of middle school, the drama of high school, and the questions of college together. Over the years, we navigated loss, relationships, kids, moves, and more. Thanks for the weekly texts, our annual girls' trips, your willingness to be my guinea pigs, and the lifelong commitment to being "my people." Just remember, if you ever change your mind, I have pictures of all of you from the fashion heights of the '80s and I'm not afraid to use them.

Nadine (Nay-Nay), I know neither of us imagined nor would have chosen the circumstances that ultimately lead to our lives colliding. *But if we only look at what's missing, we fail to see what is there.* Thank you for your constant encouragement and support. I'm so grateful we're family.

Katherine, thank you for coaching me to a place of truly embracing my purpose and values in all their *uncomfortable* glory. This book couldn't exist without you!

To the Northfield Publishing team: Thank you for believing in the message of embracing uncomfortable. John, thanks for championing this book and patiently answering my many questions as a first-time solo author. Betsey, thank you for your wisdom and expertise in editing this book. While change can be uncomfortable, you made embracing the edits easy.

To my clients: Thank you for your bravery. Every day you make the choice to embrace uncomfortable by stepping into vulnerable spaces, confronting unbelievable challenges, and deciding to pursue your deepest values and purpose. I am consistently in awe of the honor to be a small part of your journeys.

NOTES

Chapter 1: The Comfort Myth

1. *When Harry Met Sally*, directed by Rob Reiner (Los Angeles: Columbia Pictures, 1989).
2. Jan Hofer and Holder Busch, "Citizen Kane Was Unhappy: Motive-Goal Incongruence," *Social & Personality Psychology Compass* 11, no. 8 (2017): e12330, DOI:10.1111/spc3.12330.
3. Adapted from *Merriam-Webster's Collegiate Dictionary*, 11th ed. (Springfield, MA: Merriam-Webster, 2003). See also John Sommers-Flanagan and Rita Sommers-Flanagan, *Counseling and Psychotherapy Theories in Context and Practice: Skills, Strategies, and Techniques* (Hoboken, NJ: John Wiley & Sons, 2015).
4. According to research collected by the Statistic Brain Institute at the University of Scranton in 2018.

Chapter 2: Driving After What's Important

1. *Gremlins*, directed by Joe Dante (Los Angeles: Warner Bros., 1984).
2. Interestingly, there is this one daredevil who climbs mountains with no harness because part of his amygdala doesn't work. Glenn T. Stanton, "Watch This Dude Climb 3,200 Feet of Granite with No Harness in 'Free Solo,'" *The Federalist*, December 19, 2018, https://thefederalist.com/2018/12/19/watch-dude-climb-3200-feet-granite-no-harness-free-solo/.
3. *How to Lose a Guy in 10 Days*, directed by Donald Petrie (Los Angeles: Paramount Pictures, 2003).

Chapter 3: The Power to Choose

1. Hunter S. Thompson, "A Man Has to Be Something; He Has to Matter," in *Letters of Note: An Eclectic Collection of Correspondence Deserving of a Wider Audience*, comp. Shaun Usher (San Francisco: Chronicle Books LLC, 2013).

2. Mellody Hobson, "Color Blind or Color Brave," filmed March 2014 in Vancouver, Canada, TED video, 14:037, https://www.ted.com/talks/mellody_hobson_color_blind_or_color_brave?language=en.

Chapter 5: The Disciplined Pursuit of Pausing in a World Full of "Go"

1. If you're curious, just hop on Pinterest and search for "dopamine tattoos." Dopamine is killing the neurotransmitter popularity game.
2. Kerry Patterson, Joseph Grenny, Ron McMillan, and Al Switzer, *Crucial Conversations* (New York: McGraw-Hill, 2004), 44.
3. Greg McKeown, *Essentialism: The Disciplined Pursuit of Less* (New York: Crown Business, 2014).

Chapter 7: Balancing Feelings and Facts

1. Paris Schutz, "Great Lakes Funding Threatened," WTTW, https://news.wttw.com/2017/03/13/great-lakes-funding-threatened (accessed July 18, 2019).
2. Marsha M. Linehan, *DBT Skills Training Manual*, 2nd ed. (New York: Guilford Press, 2014).

Chapter 8: Justification, Minimization, and Denial

1. Melanie Curtin, "Are You on Your Phone Too Much? The Average Person Spends This Many Hours on It Every Day," Inc.com, October 30, 2018, https://www.inc.com/melanie-curtin/are-you-on-your-phone-too-much-average-person-spends-this-many-hours-on-it-every-day.html.

Chapter 10: The Closing Chapter—Keep the Door Open

1. Hazel Rose Markus and Shinobu Kitayama, "The Cultural Psychology of Personality," *Journal of Cross-Cultural Psychology* 29, no. 1 (1998): 63–87, https://doi.org/10.1177/0022022198291004; Vaunne Ma and Thomas J. Schoeneman, "Individualism Versus Collectivism: A Comparison of Kenyan and American Self-Concepts," *Basic and Applied Social Psychology* 19, no. 2 (1997): 261–73, https://doi.org/10.1207/s15324834basp1902_7.

ABOUT THE AUTHOR

D R. DEB GORTON earned both her MA in Psychology and her PhD in Clinical Psychology from Fuller Graduate School of Psychology in Pasadena, CA. Additionally, she holds an MA in Theology from Fuller Theological Seminary. Currently she serves as the Gary Chapman (yes, THE "Love Languages" guy) Chair for Marriage and Family Ministry and Counseling at Moody Theological Seminary as well the Program Director for Moody's Masters in Clinical Mental Health Counseling Program.

Deb currently resides in Chicago, loves the Cubs, the city's architecture, and, believe it or not, public transportation. If she's not home in the city or traveling for work, you're likely to find her with family in Colorado, Arizona, or Oklahoma (family never makes it easy, do they?!).

RECLAIM YOUR HEADSPACE AND FIND YOUR ONE TRUE VOICE

The Voices Model helps you find your one true voice. J. S. Park identifies the false voices we listen to as four inner and four outer voices. In *The Voices We Carry* you'll learn how to identify and silence these voices so you can grow fully and freely.

978-0-8024-1989-7 | also available as an eBook

SIMPLE IDEAS, LASTING LOVE.

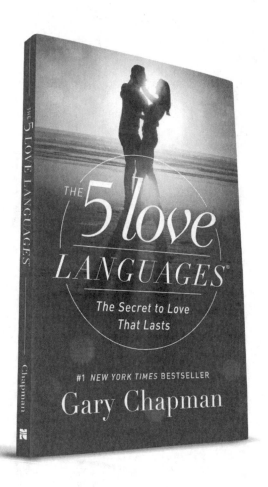

Discover the secret that has transformed millions of relationships worldwide. Whether your relationship is flourishing or failing, Dr. Gary Chapman's proven approach to showing and receiving love will help you experience deeper and richer levels of intimacy with your partner—starting today.

978-0-8024-1270-6 | also available as eBook and audiobook